Knitted Toy Tales

Percy Pig loves shopping, while Penny loves to bake,
Pickle Pig likes playing games and eating lots of cake.

Knitted Toy Tales
Irresistible characters for all ages

LAURA LONG

David and Charles

www.rucraft.co.uk

Dear Mum
Thank you for all your help. I couldn't have done it without you.

Love Laura x

Printed in China by R R Donnelley
for David & Charles
Brunel House   Newton Abbot   Devon

Commissioning Editor: Jennifer Fox-Proverbs
Editor: Bethany Dymond
Assistant Editor: Kate Nicholson
Project Editor: Nicola Hodgson
Art Editors: Prudence Rogers and Sarah Clark
Designers: Sabine Eulau and Sarah Underhill
Production Controllers: Beverley Richardson and Alison Smith
Photographer: Sian Irvine
Illustrator: Ethan Danielson

Visit our website at www.davidandcharles.co.uk

David & Charles books are available from all good bookshops; alternatively you can contact our Orderline on 0870 9908222 or write to us at FREEPOST EX2 110, D&C Direct, Newton Abbot, TQ12 4ZZ (no stamp required UK only); US customers call 800-289-0963 and Canadian customers call 800-840-5220.

Contents

Introduction

We all have moments that we cherish forever; stories we were told and childhood games that we played. Toys and fairytales were an important part of my childhood and there are certain toys I will never forget. In fact, I still have toys I could never be parted from. This collection of sweet little knitted toys brings out the child in all of us. By creating traditional toys out of yarn you can make beautiful pieces that can be enjoyed for many years to come.

Each toy in this book has its own unique character, and each has a little story to tell, a story that links all the characters together. Everyone loves stories, and you can bring a story to life with each piece you make.

There are projects in this book for everyone to enjoy knitting, from beginners to more advanced knitters and through to people like my mother, who can knit just about anything! If you are a beginner, I would advise starting with a simple project such as the bunnies (pp. 10-13) or the mice (pp. 62-67). Once you have mastered simple shaping techniques such as knitting two stitches together (k2tog) to decrease stitches, and knitting into the front and back of a stitch (kfb) to increase stitches, you can knit toys to your heart's content. You can make a whole toybox full!

I am not a fan of knitting lots of components for each toy and having to sew them together afterwards. I like to see the toy develop as it is being knitted. Therefore, my patterns have been created with shaping and using a minimal number of parts. This gives you a three-dimensional effect without all the sewing.

Frederick Frog is a very happy frog with lots and lots of friends.

Toys are perfect for using up leftover yarns. You can be creative with your yarn and colour choice. If you want to make a purple rabbit, a fluffy orange bear or a pink sparkly snake, go ahead and knit one ... in fact, knit two, three or even four! Knit a whole family of brightly coloured creatures.

You don't always need to worry about the gauge (tension) of the knitting. Who cares if your toy is a bit bigger or smaller than mine? Knitting should be fun, and mistakes give your toy personality. Imperfections should be enjoyed. No one is perfect and neither should your toys be.

Quite a few of the projects combine knitting with fabric detailing, such as fabric sewn under the birds' wings (pp. 14-21) or in the teddy bears' ears (pp. 36-41). I think this adds a special character to the toys and brings out the nostalgic nature of the work. Over the years I have collected large amounts of fabrics. Some are truly cherished pieces, and I wait for the perfect project to use them. These toys provided me with the perfect excuse to use these special fabrics, because a special toy deserves a special finishing touch. You could use fabric from an old dress, a childhood blanket, or even an old handkerchief. Make a toy that is truly personal to you; a toy that has some history and a story to tell.

I have thoroughly enjoyed working on this book, from drawing my initial sketches of the characters, to realizing them into final pieces. I hope you will enjoy knitting them as much as I have enjoyed creating them.

A cherished toy is remembered forever.

Love, Laura

The Bunny Bunch

Rating 🐝

This simple project is just right to get a beginner started on making toys

Two little baby bunnies and their mummy live in Polly Dolly's garden and sleep in a big wooden hutch. They love to jump and play silly games. They like chasing butterflies and eating dandelions and daisies.

The bunnies' heads and bodies are made in one piece from very soft, towelling-type yarn. The boy bunny has a white muzzle, so you will have to change colours to make him. Fluffy pompoms make the bunnies' tails, and fabric scraps line their ears. They are perfect projects for beginners as they introduce you to very simple shaping.

yarn
Lightweight (DK) 100% polyester with towelling or chenille texture
Mummy bunny – 1 x 1¾oz (50g) ball in white (**A**)
Baby boy bunny – 1 x 1¾oz (50g) ball in white (**A**), 1 x 1¾oz (50g) ball in pale blue (**B**)
Baby girl bunny – 1 x 1¾oz (50g) ball in pale pink (**C**)

needles
Size 6 (4mm) knitting needles

gauge
16 sts and 31 rows to 4in (10cm)
Don't worry if the gauge is not exact – it doesn't matter if the bunnies are a little bigger or smaller than shown

finished size
Mummy bunny – 5½in (14cm) long (not including tail) and 4¼in (11cm) tall
Baby bunnies – 3½in (9cm) long (not including tail) and 3½in (9cm) tall

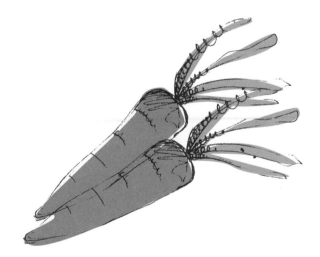

Three little bunnies live in a hutch,
They're cuddly and fluffy and soft to touch.
There's Flopsy, Mopsy and Jemima their mummy.
They hop round the garden when the weather is sunny.

Baby bunnies pattern

HEAD AND BODY

Cast on 5 sts in **yarn A** if you are knitting the boy bunny or **yarn C** if knitting the girl bunny, using size 6 (4mm) knitting needles.

Row 1 [kfb] 4 times, k1. 9 sts.
Row 2 P.
Row 3 [kfb, k1] 4 times, k1. 13 sts.
Row 4 P.
Row 5 [kfb, k1, kfb] 4 times, k1. 21 sts.
Row 6 P.
Change to **yarn B** if knitting the boy bunny and continue knitting in **yarn C** if you are knitting the girl bunny.
Row 7 [kfb, k3, kfb] 4 times, k1. 29 sts.
Row 8 P.
Row 9 [kfb, k5, kfb] 4 times, k1. 37 sts.
Row 10 P.
Cont in st st for 4 rows.
Row 15 [kfb, k7, kfb] 4 times, k1. 45 sts.
Row 16 P.
Cont in st st for 8 rows.
Row 25 [k2tog, k7, skpo] 4 times, k1.
Row 26 P.
Row 27 [k2tog, k5, skpo] 4 times, k1.
Row 28 P.
Row 29 [k2tog] rep to last st, k1.
Row 30 P.
Row 31 [k2tog] rep to last st, k1.
Row 32 P.
Thread yarn through rem sts.

EARS (MAKE 2)

Cast on 3 sts in **yarn B** for the boy bunny or **yarn C** for the girl bunny, using size 6 (4mm) knitting needles.

Row 1 Kfb, kfb, k1. 5 sts.
Row 2 P.
Row 3 K1, kfb, kfb, k2. 7 sts.
Row 4 P.
Cont in st st for 12 rows.
Row 17 K2, k3tog, k2. 5 sts.
Row 18 P.
Row 19 K.
Row 20 P.
Thread yarn through rem sts.

Mummy bunny pattern

HEAD AND BODY

Cast on 9 sts using **yarn A** and size 6 (4mm) knitting needles.

Row 1 [kfb, k1] 4 times, k1. 13 sts.
Row 2 P.
Row 3 [kfb, k1, kfb] 4 times, k1. 21 sts.
Row 4 P.
Row 5 [kfb, k3, kfb] 4 times, k1. 29 sts.
Row 6 P.
Row 7 [kfb, k5, kfb] 4 times, k1. 37 sts.
Row 8 P.
Row 9 [kfb, k7, kfb] 4 times, k1. 45 sts.
Row 10 P.
Row 11 [kfb, k9, kfb] 4 times, k1. 53 sts.
Row 12 P.
Cont in st st for 8 rows.
Row 21 [k2tog, k9, skpo] 4 times, k1. 45 sts.
Row 22 P.
Row 23 [k2tog, k7, skpo] 4 times, k1. 37 sts.
Row 24 P.
Row 25 K.
Row 26 P.
Row 27 [kfb, k7, kfb] 4 times, k1. 45 sts.
Row 28 P.
Row 29 [kfb, k9, kfb] 4 times, k1. 53 sts.
Row 30 P.
Row 31 [kfb, k11, kfb] 4 times, k1. 61 sts.
Row 32 P.
Cont in st st for 12 rows.
Row 45 [k2tog, k11, skpo] 4 times, k1.
Row 46 P.
Row 47 [k2tog, k9, skpo] 4 times, k1.
Row 48 P.
Row 49 [k2tog, k7, skpo] 4 times, k1.
Row 50 P.
Row 51 [k2tog] rep to last st, k1.
Row 52 P.
Row 53 [k2tog] rep to last st, k1.
Row 54 P.
Thread yarn through rem sts.

EARS (MAKE 2)

Cast on 5 sts using **yarn A** and size 6 (4mm) knitting needles.

Row 1 K1, kfb, kfb, k2.
Row 2 P.
Row 3 K2, kfb, kfb, k3.
Row 4 P.
Row 5 K3, kfb, kfb, k4. 11 sts.
Row 6 P.

Work in st st for 20 rows.
Row 27 K4, k3tog, k4.
Row 28 P.
Row 29 K.
Row 30 P.
Row 31 K3, k3tog, k3.
Row 32 P.
Bind off.

MAKING UP

Fold the bunny in half with knit sides (right sides) together. Sew up from each end, leaving a gap of approx. ¾in (2cm) in the middle. Turn the bunny the right way out so the knit sides (right sides) are on the outside. Fill with stuffing. Sew up the gap.

EARS

Cut out two iron-on interfacing-lined fabric ears (see p. 116 for template). Use two pieces of iron-on interfacing on each ear to make them more rigid. Sew each piece of fabric to the inside of the knitted ear (see p. 113). Stitch the ears to each side of the bunny's head, using the shaping at the top of the head to position them correctly and evenly apart.

FINISHING TOUCHES

Embroider the nose in pink or white yarn and the eyes and mouth in brown or black yarn (as shown in the photograph). Make a pompom tail (see p. 115 for instructions and p. 116 for template) using white yarn and attach to the bottom of the bunny.

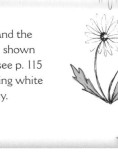

Bertie and Beatrice the Birds

Rating 🐝 🐝

The birds are made up of several small, shaped pieces and involve some intarsia colourwork

Bertie and Beatrice love to sing, so they sing all day and night. The problem is they only know one song. Is there anyone who can teach them a new one? Two songs are so much better than one!

These bright little birds are made in pure wool yarn in strong, bold colours with little embroidered details. You can make your birds in one colour if you prefer. The birds' legs are made from crocheted chains.

yarn
Lightweight (DK) 100% wool
1 x 1¾oz (50g) ball in pink (**A**)
1 x 1¾oz (50g) ball in yellow (**B**)
1 x 1¾oz (50g) ball in blue (**C**)

needles
Size 6 (4mm) knitting needles
Size E4 (3.5mm) crochet hook

gauge
22 sts and 30 rows to 4in (10cm)
Don't worry if the gauge is not exact – it doesn't matter if the birds are a little bigger or smaller than shown

finished size
Approx. 8in (20cm) long and 4in (10cm) tall

Bertie and Beatrice are songbirds,
Who twitter and tweet all day.
They have feathers so bright and beautiful,
You can see them from miles away.

• The colourwork for this project is done using the intarsia method (see p. 108). When knitting using two colours, make sure you wrap the yarns around one another when changing from one colour to the next. This prevents holes appearing between colours.

• For this pattern I have written instructions for Beatrice. She has a pink body, a yellow chest and blue wings. To make Bertie, substitute the colours so that:

yarn A = blue

yarn B = yellow

yarn C = green

Bird pattern

HEAD AND BODY

Cast on 9 sts using **yarn A** and size 6 (4mm) knitting needles.

Row 1 [kfb, k1] to last st, k1.
Row 2 P.
Row 3 [kfb, k1, kfb] to last st, k1.
Row 4 P.
Row 5 [kfb, k3, kfb] to last st, k1.
Row 6 P.
Row 7 [kfb, k5, kfb] to last st, k1.
Row 8 P.
Row 9 [kfb, k7, kfb] to last st, k1. 45 sts.
Row 10 P.
Cont in st st for 10 rows.
Beg the colour changes:
Row 21 A k16, **B** k13, **A** k16.
Row 22 A p15, **B** p15, **A** p15.
Row 23 A k2tog, k7, skpo, k2tog, k1, **B** k17, **A** k1, skpo, k2tog, k7, skpo. 39 sts.
Row 24 A p10, **B** p19, **A** p10.
Row 25 A k2tog, k5, skpo, k1, **B** k19, **A** k1, k2tog, k5, skpo. 35 sts.
Row 26 A p8, **B** p19, **A** p8.
Row 27 A k8, [**B** k1, kfb] 9 times, k1, **A** k8. 44 sts.
Row 28 A p8, **B** p28, **A** p8.
Row 29 A k8, **B** k28, **A** k8.
Row 30 A p8, **B** p28, **A** p8.
Row 31 A k8, **B** k28, **A** k8.
Row 32 A p8, **B** p28, **A** p8.
Row 33 A k8, **B** k1, kfb, k10, kfb, k1, kfb, k10, kfb, k2, **A** k8. 48 sts.
Row 34 A p8, **B** p32, **A** p8.
Row 35 A k8, **B** k1, kfb, k12, kfb, k1, kfb, k12, kfb, k2, **A** k8. 52 sts.
Row 36 A p8, **B** p36, **A** p8.
Row 37 A k8, **B** k36, **A** k8.
Row 38 A p8, **B** p36, **A** p8.

Row 39 A k1, kfb, k3, kfb, k2, **B** k2, skpo, k11, skpo, k2, k2tog, k11, k2tog, k2, **A** k1, kfb, k3, kfb, k2.
Row 40 A p10, **B** p32, **A** p10.
Row 41 A k1, kfb, k5, kfb, k2, **B** k2, skpo, k9, skpo, k2, k2tog, k9, k2tog, k2 **A** k1, kfb, k5, kfb, k2.
Row 42 A p12, **B** p28, **A** p12.
Row 43 A k1, kfb, k7, kfb, k2, **B** k2, skpo, k7, skpo, k2, k2tog, k7, k2tog, k2 **A** k1, kfb, k7, kfb, k2.
Row 44 A p14, **B** p24, **A** p14.
Row 45 A k1, kfb, k9, kfb, k2, **B** k2, skpo, k5, skpo, k2, k2tog, k5, k2tog, k2 **A** k1, kfb, k9, kfb, k2.
Row 46 A p16, **B** p20, **A** p16.
Row 47 A k1, kfb, k11, kfb, k2 **B** k2, skpo, k1, skpo, skpo, k2, k2tog, k2tog, k1, k2tog, k2, **A** k1, kfb, k11, kfb, k2.
Row 48 A p18, **B** p14, **A** p18.
Row 49 A k1, kfb, k16, [**B** k2tog] 7 times, **A** k16, kfb, k1.
Row 50 A p19, **B** p2tog, p3tog, p2tog, **A** p19.
Row 51 A k1, kfb, k17, k3tog, k17, kfb, k1.
Row 52 P.
Row 53 K1, kfb, k11, [k2tog] 3 times, k3tog, [k2tog] 3 times, k11, kfb, k1.
Row 54 P.
Bind off.

RIGHT WING

Cast on 3 sts using **yarn C** and size 6 (4mm) knitting needles.
Row 1 Kfb, kfb, k1.
Row 2 P.
Row 3 K1, kfb, kfb, k2.
Row 4 P.
Row 5 K2, kfb, kfb, k3.
Row 6 P.
Row 7 K3, kfb, kfb, k4.
Row 8 P.
Cont in st st for 6 rows.
Row 15 K2tog, k to end.
Row 16 P.
Row 17 K2tog, k to end.
Row 18 P.
Bind off.

LEFT WING
Follow instructions for right wing until row 15:
Row 15 K to last 2 sts, k2tog.
Row 16 P.
Row 17 K to last 2 sts, k2tog.
Row 18 P.
Bind off.

BEAK (MAKE 2 PIECES)
Cast on 3 sts using **yarn B** and size 6 (4mm)
knitting needles.
Row 1 Kfb, kfb, k1.
Row 2 P.
Row 3 K1, kfb, kfb, k2.
Row 4 P.

Row 5 K2, kfb, kfb, k3.
Row 6 P.
Row 7 K3, kfb, kfb, k4.
Row 8 P.
Bind off.

FEET (MAKE 2)
Cast on 3 sts using **yarn B** and size 6 (4mm) knitting needles, leaving a long piece of yarn to be used to crochet the legs.
Row 1 Kfb, kfb, k1.
Row 2 P.
Row 3 K1, kfb, kfb, k2.
Row 4 P.
Row 5 K2, kfb, kfb, k3.
Row 6 P.
Row 7 K3, kfb, kfb, k4.
Row 8 P.
Row 9 K4, kfb, kfb, k5.
Row 10 P.
Row 11 K4, skpo, k1, k2tog, k4.
Row 12 P.
Row 13 K3, skpo, k1, k2tog, k3.
Row 14 P.
Row 15 K2, skpo, k1, k2tog, k2.
Row 16 P.
Row 17 K1, skpo, k1, k2tog, k1.
Row 18 P5tog.
Cut off yarn, leaving another length of approx. 12in (30cm) to crochet the legs (the legs are crocheted with 2 strands of yarn, one length from casting on and the other from the other end of the work).

MAKING UP

BODY
Sew up from the base of the bird to the tip of her tail, leaving the top open.
Fill with stuffing.
Fold the top of the tail over to form a triangle.
The tip of this triangle should touch the top of the sewn-up base to form a V-shape.
Sew along the 'V' to close the gap.

WINGS
Cut out two iron-on interfacing-lined fabric wings (see p. 119 for template).
Sew each piece of fabric to the inside of the knitted wing (see p. 113).
Stitch the wings to each side of the bird's body using the shaping at the top of the breast to position them correctly. The fabric enables the wing to bend as though the bird is flying.

BEAK
Sew both pieces together.
Fill with a small amount of stuffing.
Stitch the beak to the bird's head using the shaping at the front of the head to position it correctly.

LEGS AND FEET
Fold the feet in half and make a crochet stitch through both sides using the leftover yarn.
Crochet a chain (see p. 114) of 10 rows with the 2 strands of leftover yarn attached to the feet.
(Using a double thickness of yarn creates a thicker leg.)
Sew round the edges of the feet.
Thread the crochet chain with foot through the base of the body.

FINISHING TOUCHES
Embroider eyes on each side of the head using brown or black yarn (as shown in the photograph).
Using a contrast-colour yarn, embroider details onto the wings.

Frederick, Polly and little mouse
love playing games

Frederick the Frog Prince

Rating 🐝 🐝

Frederick is made from two types of green yarn, and you will need to use intarsia to work the colour changes

Frederick Frog has a dream, a dream that he hopes will come true. Many years ago a wicked witch cast a spell on Prince Frederick and he has been a frog ever since. This spell can be broken only by a kiss from a beautiful girl. Every day Frederick Frog sits and dreams that a beautiful girl will come his way.

Have fun making Frederick's crown fit for a prince and decorate it with little beads to resemble jewels.

yarn
Lightweight (DK) 100% wool
1 x 1¾oz (50g) ball in variegated dark greens (**A**)
1 x 1¾oz (50g) ball in light green (**B**)
Oddment of yarn in white (**C**)
Oddment of yarn in black (**D**)

needles
Size 6 (4mm) knitting needles
You will need three needles this size

gauge
22 sts and 28 rows to 4in (10cm)
Don't worry if the gauge is not exact – it doesn't matter if Frederick is a little bigger or smaller than shown

finished size
Approx. 5in (13cm) wide and 8¼in (21cm) tall

Frederick Frog looks all around,
There's no-one about, not even a sound.
But Frederick Frog is not what he seems,
He may turn into the prince of your dreams.

• The colourwork for this project is done using the intarsia method (see p. 108). When knitting using two colours, make sure you wrap the yarns around one another when changing from one colour to the next. This prevents holes appearing between colours.

• Frederick is knitted from the head down to the legs in one piece. The arms and hands are also knitted in one piece and then attached to the body.

Frederick the Frog pattern

HEAD AND BODY

Cast on 9 sts using **yarn A** and size 6 (4mm) knitting needles.

Row 1 [kfb, k1] 4 times, k1. 13 sts.
Row 2 P.
Row 3 [kfb, k1, kfb] 4 times, k1. 21 sts.
Row 4 P.
Row 5 [kfb, k3, kfb] 4 times, k1. 29 sts.
Row 6 P.
Row 7 [kfb, k5, kfb] 4 times, k1. 37 sts.
Row 8 P.
Row 9 [kfb, k7, kfb] 4 times, k1. 45 sts.
Row 10 P.
Row 11 [kfb, k9, kfb] 4 times, k1. 53 sts.
Row 12 P.
Cont in st st for 8 rows.
Row 21 [k2tog, k9, skpo] 4 times, k1.
Row 22 P.
Row 23 [k2tog, k7, skpo] 4 times, k1.
Row 24 P.
Row 25 K.
Row 26 P.
Row 27 [kfb, k7, kfb] 4 times, k1.
Row 28 P.
Row 29 [kfb, k9, kfb] 4 times, k1.
Row 30 P.
Row 31 [kfb, k11, kfb] 4 times, k1. 61 sts.
Row 32 P.
Beg the colour changes.
Row 33 K23 in **A**, k15 in **B**, k23 in **A**.
Row 34 P22 in **A**, p17 in **B**, p22 in **A**.
Row 35 K21 in **A**, k19 in **B**, k21 in **A**.
Row 36 P20 in **A**, p21 in **B**, p20 in **A**.
Row 37 K19 in **A**, k23 in **B**, k19 in **A**.
Row 38 P19 in **A**, p23 in **B**, p19 in **A**.
Rep rows 37 and 38 two more times.
Row 43 K20 in **A**, k21 in **B**, k20 in **A**.
Row 44 P21 in **A**, p19 in **B**, p21 in **A**.
Row 45 K22 in **A**, k17 in **B**, k22 in **A**.
Row 46 P23 in **A**, p15 in **B**, p23 in **A**.
Row 47 K in **A**.
Row 48 P.
Row 49 [k2tog, k11, skpo] 4 times, k1.
Row 50 P.
Row 51 [k2tog, k9, skpo] 4 times, k1.
Row 52 P.
Row 53 [k2tog, k7, skpo] 4 times, k1.
Row 54 P.
Row 55 [k1, k2tog] rep to last st, k1. 25 sts.
Row 56 P.

RIGHT LEG

Cont on rem 25 sts as follows:
Row 57 K 12 sts and turn; cont on these sts to make right leg.
Row 58 P.
Row 59 K.
Row 60 P.
Row 61 K in **yarn B**.
Row 62 P.
Row 63 K.
Row 64 P.
Rep last 8 rows 5 more times.

RIGHT FOOT

Cont on sts for leg as follows:
Row 105 K 6 sts in **yarn A**. Fold sts in half so 1st 6 sts are facing 2nd 6 sts.
Row 106 Using a 3rd needle, knit together the 1st pair of sts, then the 2nd, and cont in this way to the end of the row. 6 sts.
Row 107 K2tog, k4.
Row 108 P.
Row 109 K1, kfb, kfb, k2.
Row 100 P.
Row 111 K2, kfb, kfb, k3.
Row 112 P.
Row 113 K3, kfb, kfb, k4.
Row 114 P.
Row 115 K4, kfb, kfb, k5.
Row 116 P.
Row 117 K5, kfb, kfb, k6. 15 sts.
Row 118 P.
Row 119 K5, skpo, k1, k2tog, k5.
Row 120 P.
Row 121 K4, skpo, k1, k2tog, k4.
Row 122 P.
Row 123 K3, skpo, k1, k2tog, k3.
Row 124 P.
Row 125 K2, skpo, k1, k2tog, k2.
Row 126 P.
Row 127 K1, skpo, k1, k2tog, k1.
Row 128 P5tog.
Tie off yarn.

LEFT LEG AND FOOT
Return to the 13 sts rem on the left side.
Row 57 K2tog, k. 12 sts.
Cont, repeating patt instructions for right leg and foot.

RIGHT ARM
Cast on 12 sts using **yarn A** and size 6 (4mm)
knitting needles.
Row 1 K.
Row 2 P.
Row 3 K.
Row 4 P.
Row 5 K in **yarn B**.
Row 6 P.
Row 7 K.
Row 8 P.
Rep last 8 rows 2 more times.

RIGHT HAND
Cont on sts for arm as follows:
Row 25 K 6 sts in **yarn A**. Fold sts in half so 1st 6 sts
are facing 2nd 6 sts.
Row 26 Using a 3rd needle, knit together the 1st pair
of sts, then the 2nd. Cont in this way to the end of the
row. 6 sts.
Row 27 K2 tog, k4.
Row 28 P.
Row 29 K1, kfb, kfb, k2.
Row 30 P.
Row 31 K2, kfb, kfb, k3.
Row 32 P.
Row 33 K3, kfb, kfb, k4.
Row 34 P.
Row 35 K4, kfb, kfb, k5.
Row 36 P.
Row 37 K4, skpo, k1, k2tog, k4.

Row 38 P.
Row 39 K3, skpo, k1, k2tog, k3.
Row 40 P.
Row 41 K2, skpo, k1, k2tog, k2.
Row 42 P.
Row 43 K1, skpo, k1, k2tog, k1.
Row 44 P5tog.
Tie off yarn.

LEFT ARM AND HAND
Follow instructions for right arm and hand.

EYES (MAKE 2)
Cast on 4 sts using **yarn B** and size 6 (4mm) knitting needles.
Row 1 Kfb in each st.
Row 2 P.
Row 3 Kfb in each st.
Row 4 P.
Cont in st st for 4 rows.
Row 9 Using **yarn C**, k.
Row 10 P.
Row 11 K2tog to end of row.
Row 12 Using **yarn D**, p.
Row 13 K2tog to end of row.
Thread yarn through rem sts, pull together to close the gap, and cut yarn.

MAKING UP

Fold the body of the frog in half with knit sides (right sides) together.
Sew up from the top of the head to the legs.
Turn frog the right way out so the knit sides (right sides) are on the outside.
Fill with stuffing.

LEGS
Sew from each end leaving a gap of approx. 1¹/₈in (3cm) in the middle. Fill with stuffing. With a few stitches, join the third and fourth dark-green stripe at the seam to bend the frog's legs at the knees.

FEET
Fold the feet in half and sew round the edges. With a few stitches, sew the frog's feet at the ankle end to his legs so they are bent at the ankle.

ARMS
Sew from each end leaving a gap of approx. 1¹/₈in (3cm) in the middle.
Fill with stuffing.
Sew on to the body using shaping to position correctly.

HANDS
Fold the hands in half and sew round the edges. Sew up gap.

EYES
Sew up eyes and fill with stuffing. Sew onto top of the head using shaping to position correctly.

FINISHING TOUCHES
Embroider the mouth in black yarn.
Make the crown out of yellow felt (see p. 122 for template). Use gold thread to embroider details or add small beads for the jewels if desired.

Babushkas

Rating 🐝 🐝

The colourwork on the babushkas is done using intarsia, which you might need to practise

The babushkas are three very pretty Russian dolls. They are good friends with Polly Dolly, but sometimes they play tricks on her by jumping and hiding one inside the other.

The babushkas are fully lined on the inside to give them some stability and to allow you to stack them inside each other, just like real Russian dolls. Each doll is decorated with different styles of flower; you can cut out pieces of felt for the flowers or embroider them.

yarn
Lightweight (DK) acrylic and wool mix yarn
1 x 3½oz (100g) ball in yellow (**A**)
1 x 3½oz (100g) ball in pink (**B**)
1 x 3½oz (100g) ball in white (**C**)
1 x 3½oz (100g) ball in red (**D**)

needles
Size 6 (4mm) knitting needles

gauge
22 sts and 30 rows to 4in (10cm)
Don't worry if the gauge is not exact – it doesn't matter if the babushkas are a little bigger or smaller than shown

finished size
Large babushka – 9in (23cm) tall
Medium babushka – 6¾in (17cm) tall
Small babushka – 4in (10cm) tall

There's Olga who's tall, and Tanya who's small,
And Nadia who fits in between.
They are three Russian dollies, who like to be jolly,
Their smiles are the best ever seen.

• The colourwork for this project is done using the intarsia method (see p. 108). When knitting using two colours, make sure you wrap the yarns around one another when changing from one colour to the next. This prevents holes appearing between colours.

• The babushkas are knitted from the head down.

Large babushka pattern

Cast on 9 sts using **yarn A** and size 6 (4mm) knitting needles.
Row 1 [kfb, k1] 4 times, k1.
Row 2 P.
Row 3 [kfb, k1, kfb] 4 times, k1.
Row 4 P.
Row 5 [kfb, k3, kfb] 4 times, k1.
Row 6 P.
Row 7 [kfb, k5, kfb] 4 times, k1.
Row 8 P.
Row 9 [kfb, k7, kfb] 4 times, k1. 45 sts.
Row 10 P.
Beg the colour changes.
Row 11 A k16, B k13, A k16.
Row 12 A p15, B p15, A p15.
Row 13 A k14, B k17, A k14.
Row 14 A p13, B p19, A p13.
Row 15 A k13, B k19, A k13.
Rep rows 14 and 15 3 more times.
Row 22 A p13, B p19, A p13.
Row 23 A k14, B k17, A k14.
Row 24 A p15, B p15, A p15.
Row 25 A k16, B k13, A k16.
Row 26 A p17, B p11, A p17.
Row 27 A k.
Row 28 P.
Row 29 C [skpo, k7, k2tog] 4 times, k1.
Row 30 P.
Row 31 [skpo, k5, k2tog] 4 times, k1.
Row 32 P.
Row 33 [kfb, k1] rep to last st, kfb. 44 sts.
Row 34 P.
Row 35 K.
Row 36 P.
Row 37 D k18, C k8, D k18.
Row 38 D p17, C p10, D k17.
Row 39 D k16, C k12, D k16.
Row 40 D p15, C p14, D p15.
Row 41 D kfb, k13, C k7, kfb, kfb, k7, D k13, kfb.
Row 42 D p14, C p20, D p14.
Row 43 D k13, C k22, D k13.
Row 44 D p12, C p24, D p12.
Row 45 D kfb, k10, C k12, kfb, kfb, k12, D k10, kfb.
Row 46 D p12, C p28, D p12.
Row 47 D k12, C k28, D k12.
Rep rows 46 and 47 5 more times.
Row 58 D p12, C p28, D p12.
Row 59 D k13, C k26, D k13.
Row 60 D p14, C p24, D p14.
Row 61 D k15, C k22, D k15.
Row 62 D p16, C p20, D p16.
Row 63 D k17, C k18, D k17.
Row 64 D p18, C p16, D p18.
Row 65 D k19, C k14, D k19.

Row 66 D p20, C p12, D p20.
Row 67 D k21, C k10, D k21.
Row 68 D p22, C p8, D p22.
Row 69 D k.
Row 70 P.
Row 71 K.
Row 72 K.
Row 73 K.
Row 74 K.
Bind off.

Medium babushka pattern

Cast on 5 sts using **yarn A** and size 6 (4mm) knitting needles.
Row 1 [kfb] 4 times, k1.
Row 2 P.
Row 3 [kfb, k1] 4 times, k1.
Row 4 P.
Row 5 [kfb, k1, kfb] 4 times, k1.
Row 6 P.
Row 7 [kfb, k3, kfb] 4 times, k1. 29 sts.
Row 8 P.
Beg the colour changes.
Row 9 A k10, B k9, A k10.
Row 10 A p9, B p11, A p9.
Row 11 A k8, B k13, A k8.
Row 12 A p8, B p13, A p8.
Rep rows 11 and 12 3 more times.
Row 19 A k9, B k11, A k9.
Row 20 A p10, B p9, A p10.
Row 21 A k11, B k7, A k11.
Row 22 A p.
Row 23 [skpo, k3, k2tog] 4 times, k1.
Row 24 P.
Row 25 C [k1, kfb] rep to last st, k1. 31 sts.
Row 26 P.
Row 27 K.
Row 28 P.
Row 29 D k13, C k5, D k13.
Row 30 D p12, C p7, D p12.
Row 31 D kfb, k10, C k3, kfb, kfb, k4, D k10, kfb.
Row 32 D p11, C p13, D p11.
Row 33 D k10, C k15, D k10.
Row 34 D p9, C p17, D p9.
Row 35 D kfb, k8, C k7, kfb, kfb, k8, D k8, kfb.
Row 36 D p10, C p19, D p10.
Row 37 D k10, C k19, D k10.
Rep row 36 and 37 3 more times.
Row 44 D p10, C p19, D p10.
Row 45 D k11, C k17, D k11.
Row 46 D p12, C p15, D p12.
Row 47 D k13, C k13, D k13.
Row 48 D p14, C p11, D p14.
Row 49 D k15, C k9, D k15.

Olga and Nadia are happy little dolls...

Row 50 D p16, C p7, D p16.
Row 51 D k.
Row 52 P.
Row 53 K.
Row 54 K.
Row 55 K.
Row 56 K.
Bind off.

Small babushka pattern

Cast on 5 sts using **yarn A** and size 6 (4mm) knitting needles.
Row 1 [kfb] 4 times, k1. 9 sts.
Row 2 P.
Row 3 [kfb, k1, kfb] 3 times. 15 sts.
Row 4 P.
Beg the colour changes.
Row 5 A k6, B k3, A k6.
Row 6 A p5, B p5, A p5.
Row 7 A k4, B k7, A k4.
Row 8 A p4, B p7, A p4.
Row 9 A k4, B k7, A k4.
Row 10 A p5, B p5, A p5.
Row 11 A k6, B k3, A k6.
Row 12 A p.
Row 13 C k1, [kfb, k2] 4 times, kfb, k1.
Row 14 P.
Row 15 D k8, C k4, D k8.
Row 16 D p7, C p6, D p7.
Row 17 D k6, C k8, D k6.
Row 18 D p5, C p10, D p5.
Row 19 D kfb, k4, C k4, kfb, k5 D k4, kfb.
Row 20 D p6, C p11, D p6.
Row 21 D k6, C k11, D k6.
Row 22 D p6, C p11, D p6.
Row 23 D k6, C k11, D k6.
Row 24 D p6, C p11, D p6.
Row 25 D k7, C k9, D k7.
Row 26 D p8, C p7, D p8.
Row 27 D k9, C k5, D k9.
Row 28 D p10, C p3, D p10.
Row 29 D k.
Row 30 P.
Row 31 P.
Row 32 P.
Bind off.

MAKING UP

Before sewing up the back of the body it is easier to embroider all the details.

FACE
Using brown yarn, embroider round the edge of the babushka's pink face.
Embroider hair, eyes and nose onto the face using the same brown yarn.
Embroider a few little stitches using red yarn for the mouth and add a few more round the top of the babushka's neck.

BODY
For the large and medium babushkas, cut out the petals, leaves and flowers from red and green felt (see p. 119 for templates).
Sew these in place (see pp. 112–113).
Add yarn details if desired.
Sew the babushkas down the back of their bodies.
Leave the bottom open.
Cut a strip of red felt and tie it in a neat bow at the front of each babushka's neck.
Neatly sew the bow to the neck.

LINING
Place each babushka on to double-thickness lining material. It is best to use T-shirt-type material as it has a bit of stretch.
Draw round the edge of each babushka, 3/16in (5mm) bigger than the doll.
Sew round the sides of this fabric, leaving the bottom open. Slip the fabric inside the babushka and neatly sew to the base of the doll. This lining enables you to fit one babushka inside the other, just like real Russian dolls.

Teddy bears' picnic...

On the first day of spring each year,

Mummy bear, Daddy bear and Baby bear have

a picnic with all of their friends.

Mummy bear bakes delicious treats for

everyone to enjoy – chocolate cakes,

cherry tarts, sweet carrot pies, and little

cheesecakes especially for the mice.

They eat lots of cake, drink plenty of tea,

and chat for hours and hours, until they

can't fit another crumb in.

Everyone enjoys the teddy bears' picnic.

Three Hungry Bears

Rating 🐝🐝

A touch of shaping makes the bears easier to sew up

Teddy bears love having breakfast parties, and the more bears you knit, the bigger the party will be! They like to have lots of different food at breakfast time, but don't forget to make plenty of porridge just in case Goldilocks comes to visit.

Knit these bears in the softest alpaca yarn you can find. Whether you're making the bears for small or big children, the luxurious feel of the yarn will offer warmth and comfort with every cuddle.

yarn
Lightweight (DK) 100% alpaca
Mummy bear – 1 x 1¾oz (50g) ball in light brown (**A**)
Daddy bear – 2 x 1¾oz (50g) balls in cream (**B**)
Baby bear – 1 x 1¾oz (50g) ball in grey-blue (**C**)

needles
Size 6 (4mm) knitting needles

gauge
22 sts and 30 rows to 4in (10cm)
Don't worry if the tension is not exact – it doesn't matter if the bears are a little bigger or smaller than shown

finished sizes
Mummy bear – approx. 12in (30cm) tall
Daddy bear – approx. 14in (35cm) tall
Baby bear – approx. 9in (23cm) tall

Mummy bear likes porridge,
Daddy bear likes honey,
Baby bear loves eggs with jelly,
which must taste rather funny.

KNITTING NOTES

Each component of the teddies is knitted separately and assembled at the end.

Mummy bear pattern

HEAD
Cast on 7 sts using **yarn A** and size 6 (4mm) knitting needles.
Row 1 P.
Row 2 Kfb to end of row. 14 sts.
Row 3 P.
Row 4 Kfb to end of row. 28 sts.
Row 5 P.
Row 6 Kfb to end of row. 56 sts.
Row 7 P.
Work 16 rows in st st.
Row 24 [k2tog, k10, skpo] 4 times.
Row 25 P.
Row 26 [k2tog, k8, skpo] 4 times.
Row 27 P.
Row 28 [k2tog, k6, skpo] 4 times.
Row 29 P.
Row 30 [k2tog, k4, skpo] 4 times.
Row 31 P.
Row 32 [k2tog, k2, skpo] 4 times.
Row 33 P.
Row 34 [k2tog, skpo] 4 times.
Thread yarn through rem sts and pull together.

NOSE
Cast on 30 sts using **yarn A** and size 6 (4mm) knitting needles.
Work 6 rows in st st.
Row 7 [k1, k2tog] rep to end of row.
Row 8 P.
Row 9 [k2tog] rep to end of row.
Thread yarn through rem sts and pull together.

BODY
Cast on 8 sts using **yarn A** and size 6 (4mm) knitting needles.
Row 1 P.
Row 2 Kfb to end of row. 16 sts.
Row 3 P.
Row 4 Kfb to end of row. 32 sts.
Row 5 P.
Row 6 Kfb to end of row. 64 sts.
Row 7 P.
Work 20 rows in st st.
Row 28 [k2tog, k12, skpo] 4 times.
Row 29 P.
Row 30 [k2tog, k10, skpo] 4 times.
Row 31 P.
Row 32 [k2tog, k8, skpo] 4 times.
Row 33 P.
Row 34 [k2tog, k6, skpo] 4 times.
Row 35 P.
Row 36 [k2tog, k4, skpo] 4 times.
Row 37 P.
Row 38 [k2tog, k2, skpo] 4 times.
Row 39 P.

Row 40 [k2tog, skpo] 4 times.
Thread yarn through rem sts and pull together.

LEGS (MAKE 2)
Cast on 25 sts using **yarn A** and size 6 (4mm) knitting needles.
Work 20 rows in st st.
Row 21 K11, kfb, kfb, k12.
Row 22 P.
Row 23 K12, kfb, kfb, k13.
Row 24 P.
Row 25 K13, kfb, kfb, k14.
Row 26 P.
Row 27 K14, kfb, kfb, k15.
Row 28 P.
Row 29 K15, kfb, kfb, k16.
Row 30 P.
Row 31 K2tog, k31, k2tog.
Row 32 P.
Row 33 [k2tog, k1] rep to end.
Row 34 P.
Row 35 [k2tog] rep to end. 11 sts.
Thread yarn through rem sts and pull together.

ARMS (MAKE 2)
Cast on 10 sts using **yarn A** and size 6 (4mm) knitting needles.
Row 1 Kfb, k8, kfb.
Row 2 P.
Row 3 Kfb, k10, kfb.
Row 4 P.
Cont in this way until 24 sts on needle.
Row 15 K.
Row 16 P.
Work 18 rows in st st.
Row 35 [k2tog, k1] rep to end.
Row 36 P.
Row 37 K2tog, rep to end.
Row 38 P.
Thread yarn through rem sts and pull together.

EARS (MAKE 2)
Cast on 26 sts using **yarn A** and size 6 (4mm) knitting needles.
Work 5 rows in st st.
Row 6 [p2 tog, p1] rep to last 2 sts, p2tog.
Row 7 K.
Row 8 [p2tog] rep to last st. P1.
Thread yarn through rem sts.

Mummy bear likes porridge ...

mmmm ...

Daddy bear pattern

HEAD
Refer to the pattern for Mummy bear's body
(see p. 38) but use **yarn B**.

NOSE
Cast on 36 sts using **yarn B** and size 6 (4mm)
knitting needles.
Work 6 rows in st st.
Row 7 [k1, k2tog] rep to end of row.
Row 8 P.
Row 9 [k2tog] rep to end of row.
Row 10 P.
Thread yarn through rem sts and pull together.

BODY
Cast on 9 sts using **yarn B** and size 6 (4mm)
knitting needles.
Row 1 P.
Row 2 Kfb to end of row. 18 sts.
Row 3 P.
Row 4 Kfb to end of row. 36 sts.
Row 5 P.
Row 6 Kfb to end of row. 72 sts.
Row 7 P.
Work 20 rows in st st.
Row 28 [k2tog, k14, skpo] 4 times.
Row 29 P.
Row 30 [k2tog, k12, skpo] 4 times.
Row 31 P.
Row 32 [k2tog, k10, skpo] 4 times.
Row 33 P.
Row 34 [k2tog, k8, skpo] 4 times.
Row 35 P.
Row 36 [k2tog, k6, skpo] 4 times.
Row 37 P.
Row 38 [k2tog, k4, skpo] 4 times.
Row 39 P.
Row 40 [k2tog, k2, skpo] 4 times.
Thread yarn through rem sts and pull together.

LEGS (MAKE 2)
Cast on 29 sts using **yarn B** and size 6 (4mm)
knitting needles.
Work 24 rows in st st.
Row 25 K13, kfb, kfb, k14.
Row 26 P.
Row 27 K14, kfb, kfb, k15.
Row 28 P.
Row 29 K15, kfb, kfb, k16.
Row 30 P.
Row 31 K16, kfb, kfb, k17.
Row 32 P.
Row 33 K17, kfb, kfb, k18.
Row 34 P2 tog, p35, p2tog.
Row 35 [k1, k2tog] rep to last st, k1.
Row 36 P.

Baby bear pattern

HEAD
Cast on 6 sts using **yarn C** and size 6 (4mm) knitting needles.
Row 1 P.
Row 2 Kfb to end of row. 12 sts.
Row 3 P.
Row 4 Kfb to end of row. 24 sts.
Row 5 P.
Row 6 Kfb to end of row. 48 sts.
Row 7 P.
Work 12 rows in st st.
Row 20 [k2tog, k8, skpo] 4 times.
Row 21 P.
Row 22 [k2tog, k6, skpo] 4 times.
Row 23 P.
Row 24 [k2tog, k4, skpo] 4 times.
Row 25 P.
Row 26 [k2tog, k2, skpo] 4 times.
Row 27 P.
Row 28 [k2tog, skpo] 4 times.
Thread yarn through rem sts and pull together.

NOSE
Cast on 24 sts using **yarn C** and size 6 (4mm) knitting needles.
Work 4 rows in st st.
Row 5 [k1, k2tog] rep to end of row.
Row 6 P.
Row 7 [k2tog] rep to end of row.
Thread yarn through sts and pull together.

BODY
Refer to the pattern for Mummy bear's head (see p. 38) but using **yarn C**.

LEGS (MAKE 2)
Cast on 19 sts using **yarn C** and size 6 (4mm) knitting needles.
Work 14 rows in st st.
Row 15 K8, kfb, kfb, k9.
Row 16 P.
Row 17 K9, kfb, kfb, k10.
Row 18 P.
Row 19 K10, kfb, kfb, k11.
Row 20 P.
Row 21 K2tog, k21, k2tog.
Row 22 P.
Row 23 [k2tog, k1] rep to last 2 sts, k2tog.
Row 24 P.
Row 25 [k2tog] rep to last st, k1.
Thread yarn through rem sts and pull together.

ARMS (MAKE 2)
Cast on 8 sts using **yarn C** and size 6 (4mm) knitting needles.

Row 37 [k2tog] rep to last st, k1.
Thread yarn through rem sts and pull together.

ARMS (MAKE 2)
Cast on 12 sts using **yarn B** and size 6 (4mm) knitting needles.
Row 1 Kfb, k10, kfb. 14 sts.
Row 2 P.
Row 3 Kfb, k12, kfb. 16 sts.
Row 4 P.
Cont in this way until 26 sts on needle.
Work 24 rows in st st.
Row 39 [k2tog, k1] rep to last 2 sts, k2tog.
Row 40 P.
Row 41 [k2tog] rep to last st, k1.
Thread yarn through rem sts and pull together.

EARS (MAKE 2)
Cast on 28 sts using **yarn B** and size 6 (4mm) knitting needles.
Work 5 rows in st st.
Row 6 [p2tog, p1] rep to last st, p1.
Row 7 K.
Row 8 [p2tog] rep to last st, p1.
Thread yarn through rem sts.

Row 1 Kfb, k6, kfb.
Row 2 P.
Row 3 Kfb, k8, kfb.
Row 4 P.
Cont in this way until 18 sts on needle.
Row 11 K.
Row 12 P.
Work 14 rows in st st.
Row 27 [k2tog, k1] rep to end.
Row 28 P.
Row 29 [k2tog] rep to end.
Thread yarn through rem sts and pull together.

EARS (MAKE 2)
Cast on 20 sts using **yarn C** and size 6 (4mm) knitting needles.
Work 4 rows in st st.
Row 5 [k2tog, k1] rep to last 2 sts, k2tog.
Row 6 P.
Row 7 [k2tog] rep to last st, k1.
Thread yarn through rem sts.

i love honey in my tummy ...

MAKING UP

HEAD
Fold the head in half with the knit sides together. Sew from each end of the head, leaving a gap of approx. 1½in (4cm) in the middle. Turn the right way so that the knit sides are now on the outside. Fill with stuffing and sew up the 1½in (4cm) gap.

NOSE
Fold the nose in half with the knit sides together. Sew up the seam starting from the tip of the nose. Turn the right way so that the knit sides are now on the outside. Loosely fill with stuffing (be careful not to overfill or the nose could look too large). Stitch the nose onto the front of the head.

EARS
Fold the ears in half with the knit sides together. Stitch around the sides from the centre of the ear. Turn the right way so that the knit sides are now on the outside. Sew along the bottom straight edge to form a double-sided ear. Stitch the ears to each side of the head using the shaping at the top of the head to position them evenly apart.

BODY
Fold the body in half with the knit sides together. Sew from each end of the body leaving a gap of approximately 1½in (4cm) in the middle. Turn the right way so that the knit sides are now on the outside. Fill with stuffing and sew up the 1½in (4cm) gap.

ARMS
Fold the arms in half with the knit sides together. Sew from the hand to under the arm. Turn the right way so that the knit sides are on the outside and fill with stuffing. Position the arms to each side of the body and sew, leaving a small gap to insert stuffing for the top of the arm. Sew up the gap.

LEGS
Fold the legs in half with the knit sides together. Sew from the heel to the top of the leg. Turn the right way so that the knit sides are on the outside and fill with stuffing. Position the legs to the base of the body and sew them on tightly.

FINISHING TOUCHES
Embroider the nose, mouth and eyes using brown yarn. Using the correct size teddy bear templates for the bear you are making (see p. 122), cut out two iron-on interfacing-lined fabric feet pads, two paw pads and two ear linings. Position them correctly and sew on (see p. 113).

Polly Dolly's Dress-up Day

See individual project patterns for more detail

Polly Dolly loves dressing up. She is really quite vain and spends a lot of time looking at herself in the mirror. She likes to wear a different dress every day of the week. On Monday she wears a green dress, on Tuesday she wears a blue dress, on Wednesday she wears a purple dress, on Thursday she wears a pink dress, on Friday she wears a yellow dress, and at the weekend she wears her favourite dresses - the red dress on Saturday and the white dress with its little flower on Sunday.

There are various elements to this project. First come the instructions on how to make Polly Dolly herself (pp. 44-47), including her hair. Then there are patterns for her outfits. On pp. 48-49 are the patterns for her red dress with blue stripes, and for her blue shoes. On pp. 50-51 are the instructions to make her white dress. Finally, there are instructions for Polly's underwear (p.51), which is sewn rather than knitted.

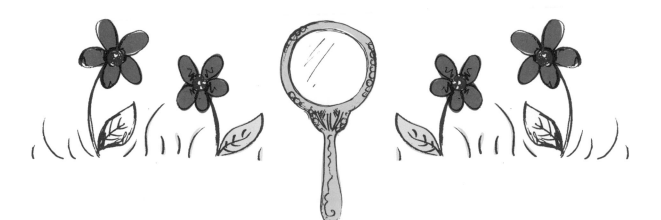

Polly the dolly has plaits in her hair,
She has beautiful dresses she loves to wear,

A red dress, a white dress all patterned with flowers,
She looks in the mirror for hours and hours.

Polly Dolly

Rating 🐭 🐭 🐭

This is quite an advanced project because of the different components involved and the importance of getting Polly's face and hair to look right

You start knitting from the top of the doll's head. The head, shoulders and body are knitted in one piece. The arms are picked up from stitches set aside while making the body. The legs are knitted separately. Take care when adding Polly's finishing touches, particularly her hair and facial features. Try to make her face look as realistic as you can, and arrange her hair into a pretty style.

yarn
Lightweight (DK) merino wool, microfibre and cashmere mix
1 x 1¾oz (50g) ball in pale pink

needles
Size 6 (4mm) knitting needles
2 stitch holders

gauge
22 sts and 30 rows to 4in (10cm)

finished size
18½in (47cm) from head to toe

Polly Dolly pattern

HEAD

Cast on 8 sts using size 6 (4mm) knitting needles.
Row 1 [kfb] 7 times, k1.
Row 2 P.
Row 3 [k1, kfb] 7 times, k1. 22 sts.
Row 4 P.
Row 5 [k2, kfb] 3 times, k3 [kfb, k2] 2 times, kfb, k3.
Row 6 P.
Row 7 K2, kfb, k3, kfb, k3, kfb, k5, kfb, k3, kfb, k3, kfb, k3.
Row 8 P.
Row 9 K2, kfb, k4, kfb, k4, kfb, k7, kfb, k4, kfb, k4, kfb, k3. 40 sts.
Row 10 P.
Cont in st st for 18 rows.
Row 29 K2, skpo, k4, skpo, k4, skpo, k7, k2tog, k4, k2tog, k4, k2tog, k3.
Row 30 P.
Row 31 K2, skpo, k3, skpo, k3, skpo, k5, k2tog, k3, k2tog, k3, k2tog, k3.
Row 32 P.
Row 33 K2, skpo, k6, skpo, k3, k2tog, k6, k2tog, k3. 24 sts.
Row 34 P.
Row 35 K.
Row 36 P.
Row 37 [kfb, k1] 5 times, [kfb] 3 times, [k1, kfb] 5 times, k1. 37 sts.
Row 38 P.

SHOULDER AND ARMHOLE SHAPING

Row 39 K7, kfb, k1, kfb, k1, kfb, k13, kfb, k1, kfb, k1, kfb, k7.
Row 40 P.
Row 41 K7, [kfb, k1] 4 times, k13, [kfb, k1] 4 times, k7. 51 sts.
Row 42 P.
Row 43 K.
Row 44 P.

BODY

Row 45 K7, put next 12 sts (for 1st arm) on a stitch holder, cast 8 sts onto 1st 7 sts, k13, put next 12 sts (for 2nd arm) on a stitch holder, cast on 8 sts to the middle 13 sts, k7.
Row 46 P across 43 sts, leaving arm sts on the stitch holders to be picked up later.
Row 47 K10, kfb, k20, kfb, k11. 45 sts.
Row 48 P.
Cont in st st for 28 rows.
Row 77 [k2tog, k7, skpo] 4 times, k1. 37 sts.
Row 78 P.
Row 79 [k2, k2tog] rep to last st, k1.
Row 80 P.
Bind off loosely.

ARMS (MAKE 2)

Pick up 12 sts from 1st stitch holder.
Row 1 K.
Row 2 P.
Row 3 Kfb, k to last st, kfb.
Row 4 P.
Cont in st st for 36 rows.
Row 41 [k2, k2tog,] 3 times, k2.
Row 42 P.
Row 43 [k1, k2tog] 3 times, k2.
Row 44 P.
Row 45 [k2tog] 4 times.
Row 46 P.
Thread yarn through rem sts.

LEGS (MAKE 2)

Cast on 17 sts using size 6 (4mm) knitting needles.
Work in st st for 50 rows.
Row 51 K7, kfb, kfb, k8.
Row 52 P.
Row 53 K8, kfb, kfb, k9.
Row 54 P.
Row 55 K9, kfb, kfb, k10.
Row 56 P.

Row 57 K10, kfb, kfb, k11.
Row 58 P.
Row 59 K11, kfb, kfb, k12.
Row 60 P.
Row 61 K2tog, k23, k2tog.
Row 62 P.
Row 63 K2tog, k9, k3tog, k9, k2tog. 21 sts.
Row 64 P.
Bind off.

MAKING UP

BODY

The head, body and arms are knitted all in one piece. Because the arms and legs are thin it is easier not to have to turn the pieces inside out to sew. Sew along the arms and fill with stuffing. Sew down the back of the body and head and fill with stuffing, leaving the bottom seam open for the legs.

LEGS

Sew down the back of the legs to the tips of the toes.
Fill with stuffing.
Sew the legs into the gap left at the bottom of the body with the leg seam at the back.

KNEES

Halfway down the leg, pull up two or three stitches using the pink yarn. Sew the yarn neatly inside the leg so that no yarn is visible.

HAIR

Use two shades of brown yarn for the hair. Wrap the yarn round a large book (the book I used was about 10½in/27cm tall). The bigger the book, the longer the hair. Continue wrapping the yarn around the book until it is approximately 2³⁄₈in (6cm) wide and ³⁄₁₆–³⁄₈in (5mm–1cm) thick. The more yarn you wrap, the thicker the hair.
Carefully stitch over and under one side of the hair then back again so that every strand of hair is captured in the stitches.
Cut the hair on the other side of the book so that there is an even amount of hair on each side of the stitches.
Position the hair at the top of the head with the stitches in the centre. Spread the hair so that it runs down the side and back of Polly's head.
Sew the hair tightly along the top of her head and round the bottom, back and sides of the head.
Every strand of hair needs to be sewn down.
Divide the hair in two and plait each side. Tie the bottom of the plaits with more brown yarn to hold them in place.

FACIAL FEATURES

Embroider the eyes using brown or black yarn (as shown in the photograph).
Using the pink yarn, pull up two stitches just below the centre of the eyes and pull tightly (just like the knees, but much smaller). This creates the nose. Sew the pink yarn neatly inside the body so that no thread is visible on the outside.
Using bright pink yarn, make two or three stitches just below the nose. This creates the mouth.

Polly Dolly's red dress and blue shoes

Rating 🐝

Polly Dolly's red dress and blue shoes are fairly simple to make

The red dress is mostly knitted in stockinette stitch, with a few contrast bands in blue and a few textured bands in reverse stockinette stitch to form a waistband and a hem. The blue shoes are worked in garter stitch. You can make any colour dress you like just by altering the yarn from the ones I have suggested. Make lots of different dresses in all shades of colours so Polly Dolly has a new dress to wear every day of the week!

yarn
Lightweight (DK) wool and cotton mix yarn
1 x 1¾oz (50g) ball in red (**A**)
1 x 1¾oz (50g) ball in blue (**B**)

needles
Size 6 (4mm) knitting needles

gauge
20 sts and 30 rows to 4in (10cm)

finished size
8in (20cm) long (not including straps)

Red dress and blue shoes pattern

DRESS
Cast on 90 sts using **yarn A** and size 6 (4mm) knitting needles.
Row 1 K.
Row 2 P.
Row 3 K.
Row 4 K.
Row 5 B k.
Row 6 P.
Row 7 K.
Row 8 P.
Row 9 K.
Row 10 A k.
Cont in st st for 24 rows.
Row 35 [k2tog] rep to end of row. 45 sts.
Row 36 K.
Row 37 P.
Row 38 K.
Row 39 P.
Row 40 K.
Row 41 K.
Row 42 P.
Cont in st st for 6 rows.
Row 49 B k
Row 50 P.
Row 51 A k
Row 52 P.
Row 53 Bind off 15 sts, k15 (work only on these middle 15 sts).
Row 54 P.
Row 55 K.
Row 56 P.
Bind off middle 15 sts.
Bind off rem 15 sts.

DRESS STRAPS (MAKE 2)
Cast on 4 sts using **yarn B** and size 6 (4mm) knitting needles.
Work in st st for 22 rows.
Bind off.

SHOES (MAKE 2)
Cast on 26 sts using **yarn B** and size 6 (4mm) knitting needles.
K 6 rows.
Row 7 K11, skpo, k2tog, k11.
Row 8 K10, skpo, k2tog, k10.
Row 9 K9, skpo, k2tog, k9.
Bind off.

SHOE STRAPS (MAKE 2)
Cast on 3 sts using **yarn B** and size 6 (4mm) knitting needles.
Work in st st for 22 rows.
Bind off.

MAKING UP

DRESS
Sew down the back of the dress.
Sew each strap to the front and back of the dress.

SHOES
Sew up the back and bottom of the shoes, attaching both ends of the straps at the top.

Polly Dolly's white dress

Rating 🐝 🐝 🐝

This dress has more detail than the red dress, so you may find it more challenging

The white dress features a lacy panel around the bottom edge. It is also decorated with a pretty appliquéd flower motif. Polly Dolly's underwear is sewn rather than knitted; use the templates on pp. 120–121 and follow the instructions on p. 51 to make the vest and knickers. We've given you a template for the flower (see p. 120), but you could add an appliqué of another pretty design if you like; maybe your Polly would prefer a butterfly or a star shape?

yarn
Lightweight (DK) merino wool, microfibre and cashmere mix
1 x 1¾oz (50g) ball in cream

needles
Size 6 (4mm) knitting needles

gauge
24 sts and 34 rows to 4in (10cm)

finished size
7in (18cm) long (not including straps)

White dress pattern

DRESS

Cast on 93 sts using size 6 (4mm) knitting needles.

Row 1 K1 [yon, sl1 purlwise, k2tog, psso, yon, k5] rep to last 4 sts, yon, sl1, k2tog, psso, yon, k1.

Row 2 P.

Row 3 K1 [yon, sl1 purlwise, k2tog, psso, yon, k5] rep to last 4 sts, yon, sl1, k2tog, psso, yon, k1.

Row 4 P.

Row 5 K1 [k3, yon, skpo, k1, k2tog, yon] rep to last 4 sts, k4.

Row 6 P.

Row 7 K1 [yon, sl1, k2tog, psso, yon, k1] rep to last 4 sts, yon, sl1, k2tog, psso, yon, k1.

Row 8 P.

Row 9 K.

Row 10 K.

Row 11 K.

Row 12 P.

Cont in st st for 24 rows, or 34 rows to make a slightly longer dress, adjusting the foll row numbers by 10.

Row 37 k3tog [k2tog] rep to end of row. 46 sts.

Row 38 K.

Row 39 P.

Row 40 K.

Row 41 P.

Row 42 K.

Cont in st st for 12 rows.

Row 55 Bind off 15 sts, k16 (work only on these middle 16 sts).

Row 56 P.

Row 57 K.

Row 58 K.

Row 59 K.

Row 60 P.

Bind off 16 sts.

Bind off rem 15 sts.

STRAPS

Cast on 3 sts using size 6 (4mm) knitting needles.

Work in st st for 24 rows.

Bind off.

MAKING UP

Sew down the back of the dress.

Sew the straps to the front and back of the dress.

Cut out iron-on interfacing-lined fabric petals (see p. 120 for template).

Sew each petal to the dress (see p. 113). You could add more flowers if you want the dress to be more decorated.

Dolly's underwear

The templates for the vest and knickers are on pp. 120–121.

KNICKERS

Using the template, cut out the knickers using T-shirt material. This stretchy type of fabric is perfect because it doesn't fray and has the added stretch that real knickers have.

Sew each side of the knickers together.

Turn the right way and sew a neat running stitch around the top for extra detail.

VEST

Using the same fabric as the knickers, cut out the vest using the template.

Sew a lace trim round the top of the vest.

Sew along the back of the vest.

Cut out two pieces of ribbon about 3 1/8 in (8cm) long.

Sew the ribbon to the top of the vest to form straps.

lovely lace

Everyone loves a bedtime story

Simon Snake

Rating 🐝 🐝

Simon's colourful patterns are made using the Fair Isle technique, which you might need to practise

Simon Snake is a very inquisitive snake. He loves to explore everything around him. He might seem scary, but he is actually a bit clumsy and not good at climbing, which is why he falls out of trees.

Simon's long, narrow body is knitted in the round using a circular needle, with double-pointed needles for the tip of the tail. You could knit his whole body in stripes if you prefer; use up the oddments in your stash.

yarn
Lightweight (DK) 100% merino wool
3 x 1¾oz (50g) balls in dark green (**A**)
1 x 1¾oz (50g) ball in blue (**B**)
1 x 1¾oz (50g) ball in pink (**C**)
1 x 1¾oz (50g) ball in red (**D**)
1 x 1¾oz (50g) ball in light green (**E**)
Oddment of white yarn (**F**)
Oddment of black yarn (**G**)

needles
Size 6 (4mm) knitting needles
Size 10 (6mm) circular needle
3 x size 10 (6mm) double-pointed needles

gauge
16 sts and 21 rows to 4in (10cm)
Don't worry if the gauge is not exact – it doesn't matter if Simon is a little bigger or smaller than shown

finished size
35¼in (90cm) long

Simon Snake lives in the trees,
He slithers along the bright green leaves.
You'd better watch out if you're below,
He'll drop on your head and land on your toe.

Simon Snake pattern

• You will be knitting
with 2 strands of yarn
throughout for the head
and body of the snake.

• You start the snake
from the straight part
of the tail end, but not
from the very end. This is
finished later.

• Stuff the snake's head
and body while you knit;
the longer the tube of the
body is, the harder it is
to stuff.

• See p. 117 for the chart
for the Fair Isle pattern
on the snake's body.

BODY
Using waste yarn, cast on 32 sts on a size 10
(6mm) circular needle.
K 4 rows.
(This provisional cast-on will be removed later.)

Change to **yarn A** using 2 strands. Cont using
2 strands for the entire snake in all colours.
Row 1 K.
Row 2 K.
Row 3 K.
Row 4 Start pattern in **yarn B** using the chart on
p. 117 (this is an 8-row pattern).
Rep these 8 pattern rows 13 times (14 colour bands
in all).
The colour order is **B, C, D, C, B, E**, repeating until
you get to the head.

HEAD (CONT FROM BODY)
Row 1 Using **yarn A** k7, kfb, kfb, k14, kfb, kfb, k7.
Row 2 K.
Row 3 K8, kfb, kfb, k16, kfb, kfb, k8.
Row 4 K.
Row 5 K9, kfb, kfb, k18, kfb, kfb, k9.
K 11 rows.

Row 17 K8, skpo, k2, k2tog, k16, skpo, k2, k2tog, k8.
Row 18 K.
Row 19 K7, skpo, k2, k2tog, k14, skpo, k2, k2tog, k7.
Row 20 K.
Row 21 K6, skpo, k2, k2tog, k12, skpo, k2, k2tog, k6.
Row 22 K.
Row 23 K5, skpo, k2, k2tog, k10, skpo, k2, k2tog, k5.
Row 24 K.
Row 25 K4, skpo, k2, k2tog, k8, skpo, k2, k2tog, k4.
Row 26 K.
Row 27 K3, skpo, k2, k2tog, k6, skpo, k2, k2tog, k3.
Row 28 K.
Row 29 K2, skpo, k2, k2tog, k4, skpo, k2, k2tog, k2.
16 sts.
Row 30 K.
Bind off.

TAIL
Unravel the waste yarn from the start of the snake
and slip the green stitches back onto the circular
needles. Make sure you start on the 1st stitch.
Keep stuffing the snake as you go along; as you knit,
the hole becomes smaller and you won't be able to
stuff it at the end.

Row 1 Using **yarn E**, k. 32 sts.
Row 2 K.
Row 3 Using **yarn A**, k.
Row 4 [k6, k2tog] 4 times. 28 sts.
Row 5 Using **yarn B**, k.
Row 6 K.
Row 7 Using **yarn A**, k.
Row 8 [k5, k2tog] 4 times. 24 sts.
Row 9 Using **yarn C** k.
Row 10 K.
Row 11 Using **yarn A**, k.
Row 12 [k4, k2tog] 4 times. 20 sts.
Row 13 K.
Row 14 K.
Row 15 Using **yarn D**, k.
Row 16 [k3, k2tog] 4 times. 16 sts.
Row 17 K.
Row 18 K.

Because you have only a few stitches now,
I would advise changing to 3 double-pointed
needles instead of the circular needle as the work
will be easier to manage.

Row 19 [k2, k2tog] 4 times. 12 sts.
Row 20 K.
Row 21 K.

Watch out for Simon Snake!

Row 22 [k1, k2tog] to end of row. 8 sts.
Row 23 K.
Row 24 K.
Row 25 K.
Row 26 K.
Row 27 K.
Pull yarn through rem sts.

EYES (MAKE 2)
Cast on 4 sts with a single strand of **yarn A** using size 6 (4mm) knitting needles.
Row 1 Kfb in each st. 8 sts.
Row 2 P.
Row 3 Kfb in each st. 16 sts.
Row 4 P.
Cont in st st for 4 rows.
Row 9 Using **yarn F**, k.
Row 10 P.
Row 11 K2tog to end of row.
Row 12 Using **yarn G**, p.
Row 13 K2tog to end of row.
Thread yarn through needle to close.

FINISHING TOUCHES
Using the template (see p. 117), cut out the snake's tongue in red felt and stitch it into the gap at the front of the head.
Close the gap with the tongue included.
Sew eyes onto the head (as shown in the photograph).
Embroider little nose details.

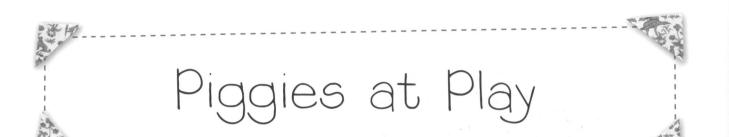

Piggies at Play

Rating 🐝 🐝

Easy to knit and assemble with minimal sewing

Percy, Penny and Pickle are very happy pigs. Percy likes going to
the market and Penny likes making cakes for her friends, the three
bears. But watch out for naughty little Pickle; he loves Penny's cakes
and when no one is looking, he will quickly gobble them all up!

Whether you make one or all three of the little pigs, choose
a dusky pink yarn for adorable results. Their cute curly tails can
be crocheted or simply plaited from the same yarn.

yarn
Lightweight (DK) merino wool, microfibre
and cashmere mix
1 x 1¾oz (50g) ball per pig in pale pink

needles
Size 6 (4mm) knitting needles
Size E4 (3.5mm) crochet hook (optional)

gauge
22 sts and 30 rows to 4in (10cm)
*Don't worry if the tension is not exact
– it doesn't matter if the piggies are a little
bigger or smaller than shown*

finished size
Approx. 7in (18cm) long and 5in (13cm) tall

Percy Pig loves shopping, while Penny loves to bake,
Pickle Pig likes playing games and eating lots of cake.

KNITTING NOTES

You start knitting the piggies from the nose, then the rest of the head, and then the rest of the body, all in one piece. The piggies' ears and legs are knitted in separate pieces and attached to the body later.

Piggy pattern

HEAD

Cast on 4 sts using size 6 (4mm) knitting needles.

Row 1 [kfb] 3 times, k1.
Row 2 P.
Row 3 [kfb] 6 times, k1.
Row 4 K.
Row 5 K3, kfb, k4, kfb, k4.
Row 6 P.
Row 7 K4, kfb, k4, kfb, k5.
Row 8 P.
Row 9 K5, kfb, k4, kfb, k6.
Row 10 P.
Row 11 K6, kfb, k4, kfb, k7.
Row 12 P.

Row 13 K2 [kfb, k4] 3 times, kfb, k3.
Row 14 P.
Row 15 K2, kfb, k6, kfb, k4, kfb, k6, kfb, k3.
Row 16 P.
Row 17 K2, kfb, k8, kfb, k4, kfb, k8, kfb, k3.
Row 18 P.
Row 19 K2, kfb, k10, kfb, k4, kfb, k10, kfb, k3.
Row 20 P.
Row 21 K2, kfb, k12, kfb, k4, kfb, k12, kfb, k3. 41 sts.
Row 22 P.
Row 23 K.
Row 24 P.
Row 25 K2, skpo, k12, skpo, k5, k2tog, k12, k2tog, k2.
Row 26 P.
Row 27 K2, skpo, k10, skpo, k5, k2tog, k10,

60

k2tog, k2.
Row 28 P.
Row 29 K2, skpo, k8, skpo, k5, k2tog, k8, k2tog, k2. 29 sts.
Row 30 P.
Row 31 K.
Row 32 P.

BODY
Row 33 K1 [kfb, k1] rep to end of row. 43 sts.
Row 34 P.
Work 26 rows in st st.
Row 61 K1 [k2tog, k1] rep to end of row.
Row 62 P.
Row 63 K1 [k2tog] rep to end of row. 15 sts.
Row 64 P.
Thread yarn through rem 15 sts and pull together to form the pig's bottom.
Leave a length of thread to sew the pig up.

EARS (MAKE 2)
Cast on 3 sts using size 6 (4mm) knitting needles.
Row 1 Kfb, k2.
Row 2 Kfb, p3.
Row 3 Kfb, k4.
Cont in this way until there are 9 sts.
Work 4 rows in st st.
Run thread through rem sts and pull up to form the base of the pig's ears.

LEGS (MAKE 4)
Cast on 16 sts using size 6 (4mm) knitting needles.
Work 14 rows in st st.
Row 15 [k2tog] rep to end of row.
Row 16 P.
Thread yarn through rem sts to close up feet.

TAIL
Use size E4 (3.5mm) crochet hook to make a chain, leaving approx. 4in (10cm) of yarn before 1st chain stitch. Work 18 chains.
Thread yarn through last sts and sew through all the chain sts until you join the initial 3in (7.5cm) of yarn at beg of pig's tail. These 2 yarns are used to sew the tail onto the pig.

Alternatively, plait 3 ends of yarn together for approx. 4in (10cm) and use this as the tail. Remember to leave some yarn at the end to sew the tail onto the pig.

MAKING UP

BODY
Fold the piggy in half with both knit sides (right sides) together. Sew from each end of the pig (his nose and bottom), leaving a gap of approx. 1½in

yum yum ... oink

(4cm) in the middle. Turn the pig the right way out so that the knit sides (right sides) are on the outside. Fill with stuffing and sew up the gap.

LEGS
Fold the legs in half with the knit sides together. Sew up from the feet using the saved yarn. Turn the legs the right way out so that the knit sides are on the outside. Fill with stuffing and sew evenly and tightly to the underside of the body.

EARS
Sew the ears onto the top of the head using the shaping as a guide to position them evenly apart.

TAIL
Sew the tail onto the centre of the pig's bottom. Twist the tail to make it curly and stitch into place.

FINISHING TOUCHES
Embroider the eyes and nose using little stitches. Using the templates on p. 117, cut out four iron-on interfacing-lined fabric feet pads and two ear pads. Position as shown in the photograph and sew on (see p. 113).

Mischievous Mice

Rating 🐭

Quick and simple to knit

These little mice are very naughty; they love to nibble on your favourite treats. They will happily eat your last cookie or slice of cake, and will even munch on the mouldy bits of cheese found down the side of your favourite armchair - yuck!

Mice are the perfect stash busters. You can enjoy creating lots of lovely mice, each using a mixture of different yarns left over from other knitted toys - this is a great chance to experiment.

yarn
Any small amounts of lightweight (DK) yarn from your stash

needles
Size 6 (4mm) knitting needles
Size 4 (3.5mm) knitting needles
Size E4 (3.5mm) crochet hook (optional)

gauge
22 sts and 30 rows to 4in (10cm)

finished size
Those shown are approx. 4in (10cm) from nose to tail
The size of your mice and the gauge will vary depending on the type of yarn used

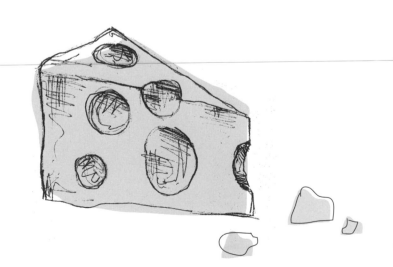

Little mice cause mischief,
running round and round,
They search for cheese and nibbles,
then hide them underground.

• You start knitting the mice from the nose all the way along to the bottom.

• To make the stripy mouse, work 2 rows in stockinette stitch in one colour and the next 2 rows in another colour. Continue this 4-row pattern throughout the mouse body. Carry the yarn not in use up the side of the work rather than cutting and rejoining yarn for each colour change.

Mouse pattern

BODY

Using size 6 (4mm) knitting needles, cast on 7 sts, leaving approx. 4in (10cm) of yarn before the 1st cast-on st. This is used for sewing up the mouse.

Row 1 K.
Row 2 P.
Row 3 K2, kfb, kfb, k3. 9 sts.
Row 4 P.
Row 5 K3, kfb, kfb, k4. 11 sts.
Row 6 P.
Row 7 K4, kfb, kfb, k5. 13 sts.
Cont in this way until there are 31 sts.
Row 26 P.
Row 27 K.
Row 28 P.
Row 29 K1 [skpo] 7 times, k1 [k2tog] 7 times, k1. 17 sts.
Row 30 P.
Row 31 K1 [skpo] 3 times, k3 [k2tog] 3 times, k1. 11 sts.
Row 32 P.
Slip thread through all 11 sts to close and pull to form the mouse's bottom.

EARS (MAKE 2)

Cast on 3 sts using size 4 (3.5mm) knitting needles.
Row 1 Kfb, k2. 4 sts.
Row 2 Kfb, p3. 5 sts.
Row 3 Kfb, k4. 6 sts.
Row 4 Kfb, p5. 7 sts.
Row 5 K.
Slip thread through all 7 sts to close and pull in to form the base of the ear.
Save approx. 4in (10cm) of yarn to sew the ear onto the body.

TAIL

Use size E4 (3.5mm) crochet hook to make a chain, leaving approx. 4in (10cm) of yarn before the 1st chain stitch.
Work 24 chains.
Thread yarn through the last sts and sew through all the chain sts until you join the initial 4in (10cm) of yarn at the beginning of the tail. These 2 yarns are used to sew the tail onto the mouse.

Alternatively, plait 3 ends of yarn together for approx. 4in (10cm) to use as the tail. Remember to leave some yarn at the end to sew the tail onto the mouse.

MAKING UP

BODY

Fold the mouse in half with both knit sides (right sides) together. Sew up from each end, leaving a gap of approx. 1in (2.5cm) in the middle. Turn the mouse the right way out so that the knit sides (right sides) are on the outside. Fill with stuffing and sew up the 1in (2.5cm) gap. Sew on the ears and the tail.

FEATURES

Wrap a different coloured yarn several times around the nose of the mouse until it is completely covered. Knot a small piece of yarn above the nose and unravel to create whiskers. Embroider small stitches for the eyes.

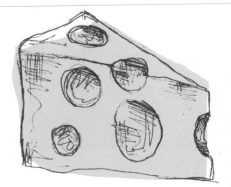

little mice running round and round ...

An exciting tale of faraway lands...

Eddie is a very happy elephant with lots of friends. He loves to tell exciting stories of his adventures to faraway lands. He has travelled from Africa to India, from America to Australia. In fact he has been to every corner of the world. Even the mice behave when he starts to talk; they keep very still so as not to frighten him. Not a sound can be heard so that not a word will be missed.

Everyone listens when Eddie talks.

Eddie the Friendly Elephant

Rating

Eddie's head, body and legs feature simple shaping, but you may find his trunk and tusks a little fiddly

Eddie Elephant is a gentle giant. He has big flapping ears to hear even the tiniest of sounds, but that doesn't stop him from getting scared. The naughty little mice always try to make him jump, and when an elephant jumps, everyone knows!

Eddie's ears and feet are lined with pretty scraps of fabric, and his tail is made from a crocheted chain. Purl ridges make the wrinkles in his trunk.

yarn
Medium-weight (aran) cotton and acrylic mix yarn
1 x 1¾oz (50g) ball in grey (**MC**)
Oddment of white yarn (**CC**)

needles
Size 8 (5mm) knitting needles
Size H8 (5mm) crochet hook

gauge
17 sts and 24 rows to 4in (10cm)
Don't worry if the gauge is not exact – it doesn't matter if Eddie is a little bigger or smaller than shown

finished size
Approx. 5¾in (15cm) tall, 9in (23cm) long and 4in (10cm) wide

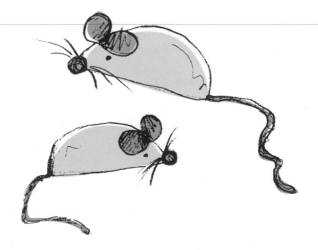

Eddie the elephant is grey and big.
He is very friendly with Percy Pig.
But Eddie Elephant is scared of mice.
They hide and jump, which is not very nice.

KNITTING NOTES

You start knitting from Eddie's trunk, then shape his head, then the main part of his body. His ears, legs and tusks are all made separately and attached later.

Eddie Elephant pattern

BODY

Cast on 3 sts in **MC yarn** using size 8 (5mm) knitting needles.

Row 1 K1, kfb, k1.
Row 2 Kfb, kfb, kfb, k1.
Row 3 K.
Row 4 K.
Row 5 P.
Row 6 K.
Row 7 Kfb, k5, kfb.
Row 8 K.
Row 9 P.
Row 10 K.
Row 11 Kfb, k7, kfb.
Row 12 K.
Row 13 P.
Row 14 K.
Row 15 Kfb, k9, kfb.
Row 16 K.
Row 17 P.
Row 18 K.
Row 19 Kfb, k11, kfb.
Row 20 K.
Row 21 P.
Row 22 K.
Row 23 K.
Row 24 K4, kfb, k4, kfb, k5.
Row 25 P.
Row 26 K.
Row 27 K.
Row 28 K5, kfb, k4, kfb, k6.
Row 29 P.
Row 30 K.
Row 31 K.
Row 32 K6, kfb, k4, kfb, k7.
Row 33 P.
Row 34 K.
Row 35 K.
Row 36 K7, kfb, k4, kfb, k8. 23 sts.
Row 37 P.
Row 38 K.
Row 39 K3, [kfb, k4] 4 times.
Row 40 K.
Row 41 P.
Row 42 K5, [kfb, k4] 3 times, kfb, k6.
Row 43 P.
Row 44 K7, [kfb, k4] 3 times, kfb, k8.
Row 45 P.
Row 46 K9, [kfb, k4] 3 times, kfb, k10.
Row 47 P.
Row 48 K11, [kfb, k4] 3 times, kfb, k12.
Row 49 P.
Row 50 K13, [kfb, k4] 3 times, kfb, k14.
Row 51 K.
Row 52 k15, [kfb, k4] 3 times, kfb, k16.
Row 53 P.

Row 54 K17, [kfb, k4] 3 times, kfb, k18. 55 sts.
Row 55 P.
Row 56 K.
Row 57 P.
Row 58 K17, k2tog, k4, k2tog, k5, skpo, k4, skpo, k17.
Row 59 P.
Row 60 K15, k2tog, k4, k2tog, k5, skpo, k4, skpo, k15.
Row 61 P.
Row 62 K13, k2tog, k4, k2tog, k5, skpo, k4, skpo, k13.
Row 63 P.
Row 64 K11, k2tog, k4, k2tog, k5, skpo, k4, skpo, k11.
Row 65 P.
Row 66 K9, k2tog, k4, k2tog, k5, skpo, k4, skpo, k9. 35 sts.
Row 67 P.
Row 68 [kfb, k1] rep to last stitch, kfb. 53 sts.
Row 69 P.
Row 70 Kfb, k51, kfb. 55 sts.
Row 71 P.
Cont in st st for 30 rows.
Row 102 [k1, k2tog] rep to last st, k1.
Row 103 P.
Row 104 [k2tog] rep to last st. 19 sts.
Row 105 P.
Thread yarn through rem sts.

EARS (MAKE 2)

Cast on 12 sts in **MC yarn** using size 8 (5mm) knitting needles.

Row 1 K.
Row 2 P.
Row 3 Kfb at beg and end of row.
Row 4 P.
Rep rows 3 and 4 until there are 20 sts.
Cont in st st for 4 rows.
K2tog at beg and end of row. 18 sts.
Bind off.

LEGS (MAKE 4)

Cast on 5 sts in **MC yarn** using size 8 (5mm) knitting needles.

Row 1 Kfb in all sts. 10 sts.
Row 2 P.
Row 3 Kfb in all sts. 20 sts.
Row 4 K.
Row 5 K.
Row 6 P.
Cont in st st for 16 rows.
Bind off.

TUSKS (MAKE 2)

Cast on 5 sts in **CC yarn** using size 8 (5mm) knitting needles.

Work in st st for 4 rows.
Row 5 K1, kfb, kfb, k2.

ssshhhh ... don't scare Eddie...

...he can hear everything with his big ears!

Row 6 P.
Row 7 K.
Row 8 P.
Row 9 K2, kfb, kfb, k3.
Row 10 P.
Row 11 K.
Row 12 P.
Row 13 K3, kfb, kfb, k4.
Row 14 P.
Row 15 K2tog, k7, k2tog.
Row 16 P.
Row 17 K2tog, k5, k2tog.
Row 18 P.
Bind off.

TAIL

Use size H8 (5mm) crochet hook to make a chain, leaving approx. 4in (10cm) of yarn before 1st chain stitch. Work 18 chains. Thread yarn through last sts and sew through all the chain sts until you join the initial 3in (7.5cm) of yarn at beg of Eddie's tail. These 2 yarns are used to sew the tail onto the elephant.

Alternatively, plait 3 ends of yarn together for approx. 4in (10cm) and use this as the tail. Remember to leave some yarn at the end to sew the tail onto Eddie.

MAKING UP

BODY

Fold the body in half with knit sides (right sides) together.
Sew from each end, leaving a gap of approx. 1¹/8in (3cm) in the middle.
Turn the right way out so the knit sides (right sides) are on the outside.
Fill with stuffing.
Sew up the 1¹/8in (3cm) gap.
Attach the trunk to the body with a few stitches.

LEGS

Fold the legs in half with knit sides (right sides) together.
Sew from the heel to top of the leg.
Turn the right way out so the knit sides (right sides) are on the outside.
Fill with stuffing.
Position the legs to the base of the body and sew them on tightly.

EARS

Cut out two iron-on interfacing-lined fabric ears (see p. 119 for template).
Sew each piece of fabric to the inside of the knitted ear (see p. 113).

Stitch the ears to each side of the elephant's head using the shaping at the top of the head to position them correctly and evenly apart.

TUSKS

Fold the tusk in half and sew along the edge.
Fill with stuffing.
Position tusks to the sides of the trunk and attach securely.

FINISHING TOUCHES

Embroider eyes above the trunk using brown or black yarn (as shown in the photograph).
Using the template on p. 119, cut out four iron-on interfacing-lined fabric feet pads.
Position correctly and sew on.

Three Little Fish

The fish are a simple shape but feature some Fair Isle and intarsia colourwork

The three little fish love to dart about in the waves. They dive deep down to the bottom of the seabed. But they had better watch out, because Peter Penguin loves eating fish for his tea!

These fish make the ideal project for using up colourful little scraps of yarn; I used yarn left over from Bertie and Beatrice the Birds (pp. 14–21). I've included some Fair Isle patterning, but you could make these fish in stripes or in plain, bright colours.

yarn

Lightweight (DK) 100% wool
I have given instructions for the fish with the blue tail. You need only small amounts of yarn in:
blue (**A**)
pink (**B**)
yellow (**C**)
green (**D**)

needles

Size 6 (4mm) knitting needles

gauge

22 sts and 30 rows to 4in (10cm)
Don't worry if the gauge is not exact – it doesn't matter if the fish are a little bigger or smaller than shown

finished size

7in (18cm) long and 2¾in (7cm) across the widest part of the body

Three little stripy fish, yellow, pink and blue,
One got caught by peter penguin, then there were two.
Two little stripy fish, having lots of fun,
One swam to deeper water, then there was one.

One little stripy fish, swimming all alone,
Was missing all his friends so he went back home.

• For this pattern I have
written instructions for
the fish with the **blue**
tail. He has a **pink** nose,
pink fins, and **green** and
yellow details. Change
the colours as you desire.

• This pattern features
both intarsia and Fair Isle
colourwork. The tail is
worked in intarsia (see
p. 108), and the pattern
around the fish's middle is
worked in Fair Isle (see
p. 109). I have written
out the pattern in
full, but there are also
templates and a Fair Isle
chart on p. 118 if you find
that easier to follow.

• The fish is knitted from
the tail to the head.

Fish pattern

BODY

Cast on 32 sts using **yarn A** and size 6 (4mm)
knitting needles.

Work in st st for 4 rows.

Beg intarsia colour changes.

Row 5 [A k2, B k5, A k2, B k5, A k2] rep to end
of row.

Row 6 [A p2, B p5, A p2, B p5, A p2] rep to end
of row.

Row 7 [A k2, B k5, A k2, B k5, A k2] rep to end
of row.

Row 8 [A p2, B p5 A p2, B p5, A p2] rep to end
of row.

Row 9 [A k2, B skpo, k1, k2tog, k2, A skpo, k1,
k2tog, k2] rep to end of row.

Row 10 [A p2, B p3, A p2, B p3, A p2] rep to end
of row.

Row 11 [A k2, B k3, A k2, B k3, A k2] rep to end
of row.

Row 12 [A p2, B p3, A p2, B p3, A p2] rep to end
of row.

Row 13 [A k2, B k3tog, A k2, B k3tog, A k2] rep to
end of row.

Row 14 [A p2, B p1, A p2, B p1, A p2] rep to end
of row.

Row 15 A k.

Row 16 P.

Row 17 [kfb, k5, kfb, k1] rep to end of row.

Row 18 P.

Row 19 [kfb, k7, kfb, k1] rep to end of row.

Row 20 C p.

Row 21 [kfb, k9, kfb, k1] rep to end of row.

Row 22 P.

Row 23 [kfb, k11, kfb, k1] rep to end of row.

Row 24 A p.

Row 25 [kfb, k13, kfb, k1] rep to end of row.

Row 26 D p.

Row 27 [kfb, k15, kfb, k1] rep to end of row. 40 sts.

Row 28 P.

Beg Fair Isle pattern.

Row 29 [B k2, D k2, B k2, D k2, B k2,] 4 times.

Row 30 [B p1, D p2, B p4, D p2, B p1] 4 times.

Row 31 [D k2, B k2, D k2, B k2, D k2] 4 times.

Row 32 [D p1, B p2, D p4, B p2, D p1] 4 times.

Row 33 [B k2, D k2, B k2, D k2, B k2] 4 times.

Row 34 [B p1, D p2, B p4, D p2, B p1] 4 times.

Row 35 D k.

Row 36 P.

Row 37 [A skpo, k16, k2tog] rep to end of row.

Row 38 P.

Row 39 [skpo, k14, k2tog] rep to end of row.

Row 40 P.

Row 41 [C skpo, k12, k2tog] rep to end of row.

Row 42 P.

Row 43 [B skpo, k10, k2tog] rep to end of row.

Row 44 P.

Row 45 [skpo, k8, k2tog] rep to end of row.

Row 46 P.

Row 47 [skpo, k6, k2tog] rep to end of row.

Row 48 P. 16 sts.

Thread yarn through rem sts.

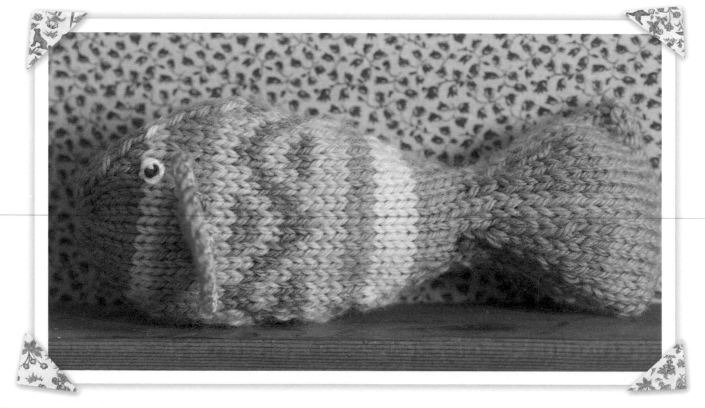

FINS (MAKE 2)

Cast on 7 sts using **yarn B** and size 6 (4mm) knitting needles.

Row 1 K2, kfb, kfb, k3.
Row 2 P.
Row 3 K3, kfb, kfb, k4.
Row 4 P.
Row 5 K4, kfb, kfb, k5. 13 sts.
Row 6 P.
Bind off.

MAKING UP

BODY

Sew the loose ends in to stop holes forming.
Fold the body in half with knit sides (right sides) together.
Sew from each end, leaving a gap of approx. 1¹/₈in (3cm) in the middle.
Turn the right way out so the knit sides (right sides) are on the outside.
Fill with stuffing.
Sew up the 1in (3cm) gap.

FINS

Cut out two iron-on interfacing-lined fabric fins (see p. 118 for template).
Sew each piece of fabric to the inside of the knitted fin (see p. 113).
Stitch the fins to each side of the fish body using the patterning to position them correctly.

FINISHING TOUCHES

Embroider eyes to each side of the head using brown or black yarn in the centre. Edge the eyes with white or cream yarn (as shown in the photograph opposite).

Peter Penguin's Fishing Trip

Rating

Peter is made up of simple shapes, but his colouring is worked in intarsia

Peter Penguin is very good at fishing. He can catch fish of all different sizes. Big fish, little fish, enormous fish and tiny baby fish ... it all depends on how hungry he is and how many friends he has round for dinner.

This is quite a simple project, although you will need to practise your intarsia technique, particularly wrapping the colours round each other where they change. Use plenty of stuffing so the penguin looks nice and plump.

yarn
Lightweight (DK) 100% wool
1 x 1¾oz (50g) ball in black (**A**)
1 x 1¾oz (50g) ball in white (**B**)
Small amount of yarn in yellow (**C**)

needles
Size 6 (4mm) knitting needles

gauge
22 sts and 30 rows to 4in (10cm)
Don't worry if the gauge is not exact – it doesn't matter if Peter is a little bigger or smaller than shown

finished size
Approx. 7in (18cm) tall

Peter penguin lives by the sea,

He dives in the water to catch fish for his tea.

KNITTING NOTES

• The colourwork for this project is done using the intarsia method (see p. 108). When changing between the black and the white yarns, make sure you wrap the yarns around one another when changing from one colour to the next. This prevents holes appearing between colours.

• Peter is knitted from the head down.

HEAD AND BODY

Cast on 9 sts using **yarn A** and size 6 (4mm) knitting needles.

Row 1 [kfb, k1] 4 times, k1.
Row 2 P.
Row 3 [kfb, k1, kfb] 4 times, k1.
Row 4 P.
Row 5 [kfb, k3, kfb] 4 times, k1.
Row 6 P.
Row 7 [kfb, k5, kfb] 4 times, k1.
Row 8 P.
Row 9 [kfb, k7, kfb] 4 times, k1. 45 sts.
Row 10 P.
Beg colour changes.
Row 11 A k16, B k13, A k16.
Row 12 A p15, B p15, A p15.
Row 13 A k14, B k17, A k14.
Row 14 A p13, B p19, A p13.
Row 15 A k12, B k21, A k12.
Row 16 A p11 B p23, A p11.
Row 17 A k11, B k23, A k11.
Row 18 A p12, B p21, A p12.
Row 19 A k13, B k19, A k13.
Row 20 A p14, B p17, A p14.
Row 21 A k15, B k15, A k15.
Row 22 A p16, B p13, A p16.
Row 23 A k.
Row 24 P.
Row 25 [k2tog, k7, k2tog] 4 times, k1.
Row 26 P.
Row 27 [k2tog, k5, k2tog] 4 times, k1. 29 sts.
Row 28 P.
Row 29 [kfb, k1] rep to last st, kfb. 44 sts.
Row 30 P.
Row 31 A k18, B k8, A k18.
Row 32 A p17, B p10, A p17.
Row 33 A k16, B k12, A k16.
Row 34 A p15, B p14, A p15.
Row 35 A kfb, k13, B k7, kfb, kfb, k7, A k13, kfb.
Row 36 A p14, B p20, A p14.
Row 37 A k13, B k22, A k13.
Row 38 A p12, B p24, A p12.
Row 39 A kfb, k10, B k12, kfb, kfb, k12, A k10, kfb. 52 sts.
Row 40 A p11, B p30, A p11.
Row 41 A k10, B k32, A k10.
Row 42 A p9, B p34, A p9.
Row 43 A k8, B k36, A k8.
Row 44 A p7, B p38, A p7.
Row 45 A k6, B k40, A k6.
Row 46 A p5, B p42, A p5.
Row 47 A k4, B k44, A k4.
Row 48 A p3, B p46, A p3.
Row 49 A k2, B k48, A k2.
Row 50 B p.
Row 51 K.

Row 52 P.
Row 53 [k2tog, k9, skpo] 4 times.
Row 54 P.
Row 55 [k2tog, k7, skpo] 4 times.
Row 56 P.
Row 57 [k2tog, k5, skpo] 4 times.
Row 58 P.
Row 59 [k2tog, k3, skpo] 4 times.
Row 60 P.
Row 61 [k2tog, k1, skpo] 4 times. 12 sts.
Row 62 P.
Thread yarn through rem sts.

BEAK (MAKE 2 PIECES)

Cast on 3 sts using **yarn C** and size 6 (4mm) knitting needles.
Row 1 K1, kfb, kfb.
Row 2 P.
Row 3 K2, kfb, kfb, k1.
Row 4 P.
Row 5 K3, kfb, kfb, k2.
Row 6 P.
Row 7 K4, kfb, kfb, k3. 11 sts.
Row 8 P.
Bind off.

WINGS (MAKE 2)

Cast on 3 sts using **yarn A** and size 6 (4mm) knitting needles.
Row 1 K1, kfb, kfb.
Row 2 P.
Row 3 K2, kfb, kfb, k1.
Row 4 P.
Cont until there are 17 sts.
Row 14 P.
Cont in st st for 8 rows.
Row 23 K2tog each end of row.
Row 24 P2tog each end of row.
Rep these 2 rows until there are 3 sts.
P3tog.
Tie off yarn.

peter penguin is very hungry...

...what size fish will he choose for his tea?

FEET (MAKE 2)
Cast on 3 sts using **yarn C** and size 6 (4mm)
knitting needles.
Row 1 Kfb, kfb, k1.
Row 2 P.
Row 3 K1, kfb, kfb, k2.
Row 4 P.
Row 5 K2, kfb, kfb, k3.
Row 6 P.
Row 7 K3, kfb, kfb, k4.
Row 8 P.
Row 9 K4, kfb, kfb, k5.
Row 10 P.
Row 11 K5, kfb, kfb, k6. 15 sts.
Row 12 P.
Row 13 K5, skpo, k1, k2tog, k5.
Row 14 P.
Row 15 K4, skpo, k1, k2tog, k4.
Row 16 P.
Row 17 K3, skpo, k1, k2tog, k3.
Row 18 P.
Row 19 K2, skpo, k1, k2tog, k2.
Row 20 P.
Row 21 K1, skpo, k1, k2tog, k1.
Row 22 P5tog.
Tie off yarn.

BEAK
Sew the two sides together and fill with stuffing.
Position the beak correctly at the bottom of the
white part of the penguin's face.
Sew on tightly.

FINISHING TOUCHES
Embroider eyes using brown or black yarn (as
shown in the photograph).

MAKING UP

BODY
Fold the body in half with knit sides (right sides)
together. Sew up from each end leaving a gap of
approx. 1¹/8in (3cm) in the middle.
Turn the right way out so the knit sides (right sides)
are on the outside.
Fill with stuffing.
Sew up the 1¹/8in (3cm) gap.

FEET
Fold the feet in half and sew round the edges.
Position feet to the base of the body and sew
them on tightly.

WINGS
Fold the wings in half and sew round the edges.
Position the wings to each side of the body just
below the neck, with the pointed part of the
wings facing downwards.

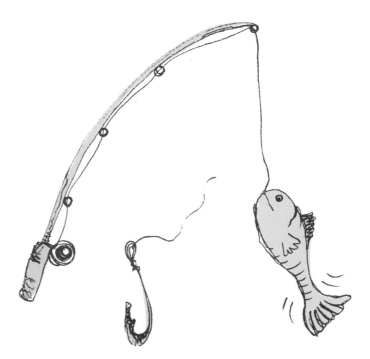

Gardening is lots of fun...

All the animals enjoy themselves in
the garden. They grow flowers of all
different colours and sizes.
There are big yellow flowers and tiny
little red flowers, all with beautiful smells
to attract the honeybees.
But most of all the animals love
to play hide and seek. They jump
in and out of the plant pots surprising
their friends. Gardening is such fun.

Hide and seek is everyone's favourite.

The Owl and the Pussycat

Rating from 🐝 to 🐝🐝

See individual project patterns for more detail

The owl and the pussycat set out on their adventures to explore the secret islands. In their boat they packed lots of lovely food and treats made by all their friends. There was a delicious cake made by the three little pigs, carrot sandwiches from the bunnies, biscuit crumbs from all the naughty little mice, and a big pot of tea from the three bears. By the light of the moon they sailed away as they waved goodbye to the animals on the sand.

There are various pieces involved in making this project. There are the owl and the pussycat, of course, and then there is their boat (pp. 94-95), complete with an anchor embroidered with their initials. The inside of the boat is reinforced with some lining material to give it some structure and help support the knitted characters.

The owl and the pussycat went to sea
In a beautiful pea-green boat.
They took some cake and lots of sweets
Wrapped up in the owl's winter coat.
They waved goodbye to their friends on the sand
And sailed towards a faraway land.

The Owl

Rating 🐝 🐝

The owl is fairly easy, although you will need to use intarsia to give him his snowy-white front

I used two shades of variegated yarn to give the owl a look of tawny feathers contrasting with his white chest. His round eyes are made out of felt and stitched on - see p. 117 for the template. Take care with the owl's finishing touches and give him beautiful big eyes. Fill him with plenty of stuffing to make his ears pointed and his belly nice and round.

yarn
Lightweight (DK) wool or wool mix yarn
1 x 1¾oz (50g) ball in variegated deep reds (**A**)
1 x 1¾oz (50g) ball in cream (**B**)
1 x 1¾oz (50g) ball in variegated bright reds (**C**)
Small amount of yellow (**D**)

needles
Size 6 (4mm) knitting needles

gauge
22 sts and 28 rows to 4in (10cm)
Don't worry if the gauge is not exact – it doesn't matter if the owl is a little bigger or smaller than shown

finished size
Approx. 8¼in (21cm) tall and 5in (13cm) wide (not including wings)

Owl pattern

EARS

Cast on 5 sts using **yarn A** and size 6 (4mm) knitting needles.
Working in st st, inc 1 st at end of every row until there are 27 sts. Slip onto a spare needle.
Rep for 2nd ear.
Slip the sts of both ears onto 1 needle.
P across all 54 sts.

BODY

Cont with the 54 sts from the ears.
Row 1 K.
Row 2 P.
Rep these 2 rows 3 more times.
Row 9 K13, skpo, k24, k2tog, k13.
Row 10 P.
Row 11 K13, skpo, k22, k2tog, k13. 50 sts.
Row 12 P.
Row 13 K13, kfb, k21, kfb, k14.
Row 14 P.
Row 15 K13, kfb, k23, kfb, k14.
Row 16 P.
Row 17 K13, kfb, k25, kfb, k14. 56 sts.
Row 18 P.
Row 19 [kfb, k12, kfb] rep 4 times.
Row 20 P.
Row 21 [kfb, k14, kfb] rep 4 times. 72 sts.
Row 22 P.
Beg the colour changes.
Row 23 K30 in **A**, k12 in **B**, k30 in **A**.
Row 24 K29 in **C**, p14 in **B**, k29 in **C**.
Row 25 K28 in **C**, k16 in **B**, k28 in **C**.
Row 26 P27 in **C**, p18 in **B**, p27 in **C**.
Row 27 K26 in **C**, k20 in **B**, k26 in **C**.
Row 28 K25 in **A**, p22 in **B**, k25 in **A**.
Row 29 K24 in **A**, k24 in **B**, k24 in **A**.
Row 30 P23 in **A**, p26 in **B**, p23 in **A**.
Row 31 K22 in **A**, k28 in **B**, k22 in **A**.
Row 32 K21 in **C**, p30 in **B**, k21 in **C**.
Row 33 K20 in **C**, k32 in **B**, k20 in **C**.
Row 34 P20 in **C**, p32 in **B**, p20 in **C**.
Row 35 K20 in **C**, k32 in **B**, k20 in **C**.
Row 36 K20 in **A**, p32 in **B**, k20 in **A**.
Row 37 K20 in **A**, k32 in **B**, k20 in **A**.
Row 38 P20 in **A**, p32 in **B**, p20 in **A**.
Row 39 K20 in **A**, k32 in **B**, k20 in **A**.
Row 40 K20 in **C**, p32 in **B**, k20 in **C**.
Row 41 K20 in **C**, k32 in **B**, k20 in **C**.
Row 42 P20 in **C**, p32 in **B**, p20 in **C**.
Row 43 K20 in **C**, k32 in **B**, k20 in **C**.
Row 44 K21 in **A**, p30 in **B**, k21 in **A**.
Row 45 K22 in **A**, k28 in **B**, k22 in **A**.
Row 46 P23 in **A**, p26 in **B**, p23 in **A**.
Row 47 K24 in **A**, k24 in **B**, k24 in **A**.
Row 48 K25 in **C**, p22 in **B**, k25 in **C**.
Row 49 K26 in **C**, k20 in **B**, k26 in **C**.
Row 50 P27 in **C**, p18 in **B**, p27 in **C**.
Row 51 K28 in **C**, k16 in **B**, k28 in **C**.
Row 52 K29 in **A**, p14 in **B**, k29 in **A**.
Row 53 K30 in **A**, k12 in **B**, k30 in **A**.
Row 54 Cont in **A**, p.
Row 55 [k2tog, k14, skpo] rep 4 times.
Row 56 Change to **C**, k.
Row 57 [k2tog, k12, skpo] rep 4 times.
Row 58 P.
Row 59 [k2tog] rep to end of row.
Row 60 P.
Row 61 [k2tog] rep to end of row.
Row 62 P.
Thread yarn through rem sts.

WINGS (MAKE 2)

Cast on 12 sts using **yarn A** and size 6 (4mm) knitting needles.
Row 1 K.
Row 2 Kfb, p11.
Row 3 K12, kfb.
Row 4 Kfb, k13.
Row 5 K13, k2tog.
Row 6 P2tog, p12.
Row 7 K11, k2tog.
Row 8 Kfb, k11.

KNITTING NOTES

• You start knitting the owl from his ears and work down towards his feet.

• The colourwork for this project is done using the intarsia method (see p. 108). When knitting using two colours, make sure you wrap the yarns around one another when changing from one colour to the next. This prevents holes appearing between colours.

Row 9 K12, kfb.
Row 10 Kfb, p13.
Row 11 K14, kfb.
Row 12 K2tog, k14.
Row 13 K13, k2tog.
Row 14 P2tog, p12.
Row 15 K11, k2tog.
Row 16 Kfb, k11.
Row 17 K12, kfb.
Row 18 Kfb, p13.
Row 19 K14, kfb.
Row 20 K2tog, k14.
Row 21 K13, k2tog.
Row 22 P2tog, p12.
Row 23 K11, k2tog.
Rep from row 8 to row 23.
Bind off.

FEET (MAKE 2)
Cast on 3 sts using **yarn D** and size 6 (4mm)
knitting needles.
Row 1 Kfb, kfb, k1.
Row 2 P.
Row 3 K1, kfb, kfb, k2.
Row 4 P.
Row 5 K2, kfb, kfb, k3.
Row 6 P.
Row 7 K3, kfb, kfb, k4.
Row 8 P.
Row 9 K4, kfb, kfb, k5.
Row 10 P.
Row 11 K5, kfb, kfb, k6. 15 sts.
Row 12 P.
Row 13 K5, skpo, k1, k2tog, k5.
Row 14 P.
Row 15 K4, skpo, k1, k2tog, k4.
Row 16 P.
Row 17 K3, skpo, k1, k2tog, k3.
Row 18 P.
Row 19 K2, skpo, k1, k2tog, k2.
Row 20 P.
Row 21 K1, skpo, k1, k2tog, k1.
Row 22 P5tog.
Tie off yarn.

BEAK (MAKE 2 PIECES)
Cast on 3 sts in **yarn D**.
Row 1 Kfb, kfb, k1.
Row 2 P.
Row 3 K1, kfb, kfb, k2.
Row 4 P.
Row 5 K2, kfb, kfb, k3.
Row 6 P.
Row 7 K3, kfb, kfb, k4.
Row 8 P.
Bind off.

MAKING UP

BODY
Fold both sides of the body together with the seam
at the back and the cream tummy at the front.
Starting from the top of each ear, sew to the top of
the back seam, then sew from the top and bottom
of each end, leaving a gap of approx. 1¹/₈in (3cm) in
the middle.
Turn the right way out so the knit sides (right sides)
are on the outside.
Fill with stuffing.
Sew up the 1¹/₈in (3cm) gap.

FEET
Fold the feet in half and sew round the edges.
Position feet to the base of the body and sew them
on tightly.

WINGS
Fold the wings in half and sew round the edges.
Pull up at the top of each wing to slightly gather.
Stitch the wings to each side of the owl's body using
the white breast to help position them correctly.

BEAK
Sew both pieces together and fill with stuffing.
Stitch the beak to the owl's head using the shaping
at the front of the head to position it correctly.

FINISHING TOUCHES
Cut out two felt eyes using the template provided
(see p. 117).
Position the eyes correctly to the owl's face using
the beak and ears to help space them evenly apart.
Stitch round the edge of the eyes using brown
thread.
In the centre of the eye, embroider pupils using
brown or black yarn (as shown in the photograph).
Use brown or black yarn to add a few stitches to
the beak to make nostrils.

The Pussycat

Rating 🐝

The pussycat is quite easy to make, but take care over embroidering her features

I made the pussycat in two shades of variegated yarn to give her the look of tabby-striped fur. Use whatever colour you like – maybe a pure black cat with green eyes, or a stripy orange one to look like a favourite ginger puss.

Pussycat pattern

HEAD AND BODY

Cast on 9 sts using **yarn A** and size 6 (4mm) knitting needles.

Row 1 [kfb, k1] rep 4 times, k1.

Row 2 P.

Row 3 [kfb, k1, kfb] rep 4 times, k1. 21 sts.

Row 4 P.

Row 5 [kfb, k3, kfb] rep 4 times, k1. 29 sts.

Row 6 P.

Row 7 [kfb, k5, kfb] rep 4 times, k1. 31 sts.

Row 8 P.

Row 9 [kfb, k7, kfb] rep 4 times, k1. 45 sts.

Row 10 P.

Row 11 [kfb, k9, kfb] rep 4 times, k1. 53 sts.

Row 12 P.

Cont in st st for 8 rows.

Row 21 [kfb, k11, kfb] rep 4 times, k1. 61 sts.

Row 22 P.

Row 23 K.

Row 24 P.

Row 25 Change to **yarn B**, k.

Row 26 P.

Row 27 [kfb, k13, kfb] rep 4 times, k1. 69 sts.

Row 28 P.

Row 29 A, k.

Row 30 P.

Row 31 B, k.

Row 32 P.

Row 33 A, k.

Row 34 P.

Row 35 K.

yarn
Lightweight (DK) 100% wool
1 x 1¾oz (50g) ball in variegated browns (**A**)
1 x 1¾oz (50g) ball in variegated bright reds (**B**)

needles
Size 6 (4mm) knitting needles

gauge
22 sts and 28 rows to 4in (10cm)
Don't worry if the gauge is not exact – it doesn't matter if the pussycat is a little bigger or smaller than shown

finished size
7in (18cm) tall and 4¾in (12cm) wide (not including tail)

Row 36 P.
Row 37 B, k.
Row 38 P.
Row 39 A, k.
Row 40 P.
Row 41 B, k.
Row 42 P.
Row 43 K.
Row 44 P.
Rep from row 29 to row 41.
Row 57 B, [k2tog, k13, skpo] rep 4 times, k1.
Row 58 P.
Row 59 [k2tog, k11, skpo] rep 4 times, k1.
Row 60 P.
Row 61 A, [k2tog] rep to last st, k1.
Row 62 P.
Row 63 B, [k2tog] rep to last st, k1.
Row 64 P. 14 sts.
Pull thread through rem sts.

EARS (MAKE 2)
Cast on 5 sts using **yarn A** and size 6 (4mm) knitting needles.
Row 1 K1, kfb, kfb, k2.
Row 2 P.
Row 3 K2, kfb, kfb, k3.
Row 4 P.
Row 5 K3, kfb, kfb, k4.
Row 6 P.
Row 7 K4, kfb, kfb, k3.
Row 8 P.
Bind off.

TAIL
Cast on 20 sts using **yarn A** and size 6 (4mm) knitting needles.
Row 1 K.
Row 2 P.
Row 3 K.
Row 4 P.
Row 5 Change to **yarn B**, k.
Row 6 P.
Row 7 K.
Row 8 P.
Rep rows 1 to 8, 4 more times.
Row 41 Change to **yarn A**, k .
Row 42 P.
Row 43 [k2tog] rep to end of row.
Row 44 [p2tog] rep to end of row.
Thread yarn through rem sts.

MAKING UP

BODY
Fold the pussycat in half with knit sides (right sides) together.
Making sure the stripes match up correctly, sew

from each end of the cat, leaving a gap of approx. 1¹/8 in (3cm) in the middle.
Turn the right way out so the knit sides (right sides) are on the outside. Fill with stuffing.
Sew up the 1¹/8in (3cm) gap.

EARS
Cut out two iron-on interfacing-lined ear pads (see p. 117 for template) and sew onto the purl side of the ear (see p. 113).
Stitch the ears to each side of the cat's head using the shaping at the top to position them evenly apart.

TAIL
Fold the tail in half with knit sides (right sides) together.
Making sure the stripes match up correctly, sew up the tail to make a tube with the shaped end closed.
Turn the right way out so the knit sides (right sides) are on the outside. Fill with stuffing.
Position the tail to the back of the cat using the seam as a centre guide.
Make a small stitch to attach the tail to the side of the cat.

FINISHING TOUCHES
Embroider the nose using pink yarn and the mouth, eyes and whiskers using brown or black yarn (as shown in the photograph). Unravel the yarn if you want to create curly whiskers.

KNITTING NOTES
• You start knitting the pussycat from her head downwards.

• The pussycat's body is worked in stripes. It's best to work these by carrying the yarn currently not being worked up the side. Avoid breaking the yarn at the end of each stripe; carrying the yarns up the side instead ensures an even, straight edge. Keep your gauge consistent and don't pull the edge too tight.

The Owl and the Pussycat's Boat

Rating 🐝

The shapes of the boat are easy to make, although you may find the anchor a little fiddly

The boat features some garter-stitch ridges to look like the planks of a rowing boat. I used variegated greens for a pea-green boat, but you could use brown yarn to make it look more like a traditional wooden sailing boat.

yarn
Lightweight (DK) 100% wool
Boat – 2 x 1¾oz (50g) balls in variegated greens (**A**)
Anchor – small amount of grey (**B**)

needles
Size 10½ (7mm) knitting needles
3 size 8 (5mm) double-pointed needles
Size E4 (3.5mm) crochet hook

gauge
14 sts and 22 rows to 4in (10cm)
Don't worry if the gauge is not exact – it doesn't matter if the boat is a little bigger or smaller than shown

finished size
Approx. 12½in (32cm) long

Boat pattern

Note that the sides and ends of the boat are knitted using 2 strands of yarn together. This creates a more sturdy boat.

BOAT SIDES (MAKE 2)
Cast on 40 sts using **yarn A** and size 10½ (7mm) knitting needles.
K 4 rows.
Row 5 P.
Row 6 K2tog, k to last 2 sts, k2tog. 38 sts.
Row 7 P.
Row 8 K.
Row 9 K.
Row 10 K2tog, k to last 2 sts, k2tog. 36 sts.
Row 11 P.
Row 12 K.
Row 13 P.
Row 14 K.
Row 15 K.
Row 16 K2tog, k to last 2 sts, k2tog. 34 sts.
Row 17 P.
Row 18 K.
Row 19 P.
Row 20 K.
Row 21 K.
Row 22 K2tog, k to last 2 sts, k2tog. 32 sts.
Row 23 P.
Row 24 K.
Row 25 P.
Row 26 K.
Bind off.

BOAT ENDS (MAKE 2)

Cast on 8 sts using **yarn A** and size 10½ (7mm) knitting needles.

K 4 rows

Row 5 P.
Row 6 K.
Row 7 P.
Row 8 K.
Row 9 K.
Row 10 K.

Rep rows 5 to 10.

Row 17 P.
Row 18 K.
Row 19 P.
Row 20 K.

Bind off.

ANCHOR BOTTOM

Cast on 4 sts using **yarn B** and size 8 (5mm) double-pointed knitting needles.

Transfer 2 sts onto the 2nd needle.

Knit in the round for 4 rows.

Row 5 [k1, kfb] twice. 6 sts.

Introduce the 3rd double-pointed needle and put 2 sts on each needle.

Row 6 K.
Row 7 K.
Row 8 K.
Row 9 [k1, kfb] 3 times. 9 sts.
Row 10 K.
Row 11 K.
Row 12 [k2, kfb] 3 times. 12 sts.

Knit 4 rows.

Row 17 [k2, k2tog] 3 times. 9 sts.
Row 18 K.
Row 19 K.
Row 20 [k1, k2tog] 3 times. 6 sts.
Row 21 K.
Row 22 K.
Row 23 K.
Row 24 [k1, k2tog] 2 times. 4 sts.

Put aside the 3rd needle and put 2 sts on the rem 2 needles.

Knit in the round for 4 rows.

Bind off.

ANCHOR TOP

Pick up 4 sts from the top of the anchor bottom (2 sts on each needle).

Knit in the round for 10 rows.

Transfer 2 sts onto a holding needle. Save these for later.

Row 11 P2.
Row 12 K2.

Rep rows 11 and 12, 10 more times.

Join the 2 sts left on the holding needle to those on the knitting needle to create a ring.

Bind off all sts, leaving length of yarn to crochet the anchor chain.

ANCHOR CHAIN

Using 1 end of yarn and a size E4 (3.5mm) crochet hook, make a crochet chain approx. 4in (10cm) long. Loop through the anchor top ring.

Tie off yarn.

MAKING UP

Sew together the bottom of both boat sides.

Sew a boat end to each end.

Cut out a 1¹⁄₈ in (3cm) wide strip of iron-on interfacing-lined fabric to reinforce the inside of the boat. Measure round the inside of the boat and cut a piece of fabric the same length. (A thick ribbon instead of a strip of fabric would work too.) Sew neatly round the inside top for an extra detail. This also adds support to the boat sides.

Attach the anchor chain to the end of the boat.

Embroider 'O&P' on the anchor using yellow yarn.

Techniques

I want all knitters to be able to experience the fun and pleasure of making their own special knitted toys, so I've included projects simple enough for beginners and more ambitious projects for knitters ready for more of a challenge. If you are just learning, or you need to brush up your skills, I've included basic techniques such as casting on, making the knit and purl stitches, and binding off. All of the toys require shaping of some sort; the methods I use for increasing and decreasing are outlined on pp. 104–106. Quite a few of the toys feature colourwork; both the intarsia and Fair Isle techniques are described on pp. 108–109. Making up the toys and embellishing them with their finishing touches will make all the difference to how your toys turn out. Take care over these details and you'll have toys to treasure for a lifetime!

Abbreviations

All knitting patterns use abbreviations to save time and space when writing out the instructions. These may seem a bit daunting if you are not familiar with the terms, but you will quickly pick up the language. Below is a list of all the abbreviations used in the patterns for this book.

approx approximately

beg beginning

CC contrast colour

cm(s) centimetre(s)

cont continue

dec decrease

DK double knitting

g gram(s)

in(s) inch(es)

inc increase

k knit

k2tog knit the next two stitches together (decrease by one stitch)

k3tog knit the next three stitches together (decrease by two stitches)

kfb knit forward and back into the same stitch (increase by one stitch)

m metre(s)

MC main colour

mm millimetre(s)

oz ounce(s)

p purl

p2tog purl the next two stitches together (decrease by one stitch)

p3tog purl the next three stitches together (decrease by two stitches)

p5tog purl the next five stitches together (decrease by four stitches)

patt pattern

psso pass the slipped stitch over (decrease by one stitch)

rem remaining

rep repeat

skpo slip one, knit one, pass the slipped stitch over (decrease by one stitch)

sl slip

sl1 slip one stitch

st(s) stitch(es)

st st stockinette stitch (stocking stitch)

tog together

yd yard(s)

yon yarn over/yarn over needle (increase by one stitch in lace pattern)

Casting on

I wanted to make the patterns in this book appealing to beginner knitters as well as to those with more experience. If you are new to knitting, or could do with a reminder of some of the main techniques, I have included instructions for some of the basics you will need to make the toys. Any project starts with casting on the stitches - this means getting the initial stitches on to the knitting needles.

There are quite a few different ways of casting on, and you may have your own favourite method. However, the knitting-on method is a simple and versatile technique.

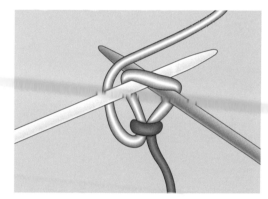

1 Make a slipknot in the working end of your yarn and place it on the left-hand needle. Insert your right needle into the loop of the slipknot and wrap the yarn around the tip of the needle, from back to front.

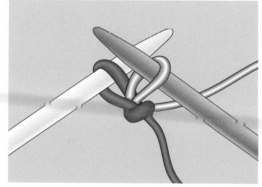

2 Slide the tip of the right-hand needle down to catch this new loop of yarn.

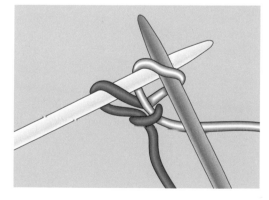

3 Place the new loop on the left-hand needle.

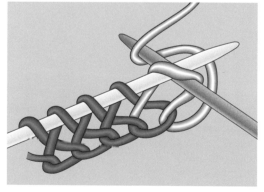

4 Repeat this process until you have cast on as many stitches as the project requires.

The knit and purl stitches

The knit stitch and the purl stitch are the two most basic stitches in knitting, but you will get a long way just knowing these two. The toys are mostly knitted in stockinette stitch (sometimes called stocking stitch by European knitters), which involves knitting one row and purling the next row.

The knit stitch

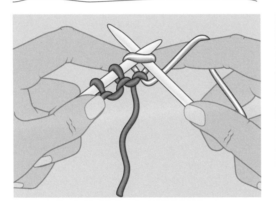

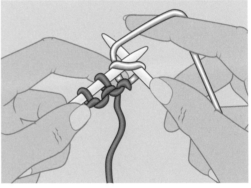

1 The working stitches will be on the left-hand needle. Take the right-hand needle and insert the tip from right to left into the first loop on the left-hand needle.

2 Wrap the yarn from back to front around the tip of the right-hand needle.

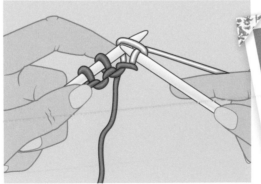

3 Slide the needle down to catch this new loop of yarn. Slip the loop off the left-hand needle and onto the right-hand needle. This is your first stitch. Repeat the process until all the stitches have been knitted off the left-hand needle onto the right-hand one.

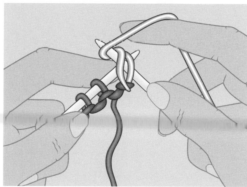

The purl stitch

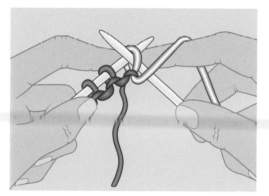

1 The working stitches will be on your left-hand needle.

2 Wrap the yarn counterclockwise around the tip of the right-hand needle.

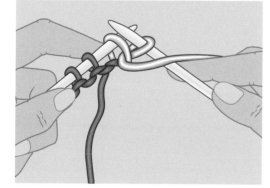

3 Use the tip of this needle to pick up the new loop of yarn. Slide the loop off the left-hand needle and onto the right-hand needle. This is your first stitch. Repeat the process until all the stitches have been knitted off the left-hand needle onto the right-hand one.

Basic stitch patterns

I have used basic stitch patterns to make the knitted toys in this book; they are mostly knitted in stockinette stitch, with a few details knitted in reverse stockinette stitch and garter stitch.

Stockinette stitch

Stockinette stitch (also referred to as stocking stitch by Europeans) is the main knitted fabric and the one that features most often in knitted designs. It is created by knitting one row and purling the next row. The knitted side forms the 'right side' or the outer side; the purl side forms the 'wrong side', or the inside.

Reverse stockinette stitch

Reverse stockinette stitch is made in the same way as stockinette stitch, but this time the purl side forms the right side. I have used reverse stockinette stitch to add a few details to some of the toys.

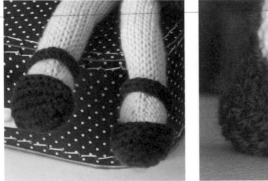

Garter stitch

Garter stitch is created by knitting every row. This creates quite a dense fabric that looks the same on both sides. Polly Dolly's shoes are knitted in garter stitch. The bottom edges of the babushkas are also knitted in garter stitch to give the dolls a firm edge around their bases.

Gauge

On the band or sleeve of every ball of yarn there is information on the gauge (what European knitters call 'tension') of the yarn. This tells you how many stitches and rows you should aim to achieve over 4in (10cm) square. The gauge will differ depending on the size of the needles you use and the thickness of the yarn. However, we all knit differently. Some people are naturally loose knitters and others knit more tightly. The beauty about toys is that the gauge doesn't really matter in most cases. If your toy is a little bit bigger or smaller than mine, who's to know! Knitting is fun and should be for everyone. The only exception in this book is with Polly Dolly (pp. 42–51); you should try to achieve the suggested gauge for both the doll and her clothes, or you may find that the clothes don't fit her properly.

Binding off

The last stage of knitting the toys will be binding off. Then you can move onto the making up!

Standard bind-off

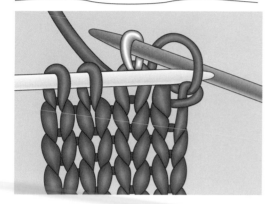 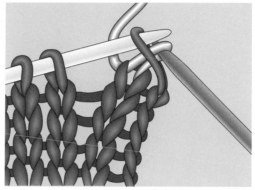

1 Work the first stitch on the left-hand needle as if making a usual knit stitch. Then knit the second stitch. Insert the left-hand needle into the first stitch on the right-hand needle.

2 Pass this over the second loop on the right-hand needle and drop it off the needle. This makes the first bound-off stitch. To continue, knit the next stitch. Use your left-hand needle to pass the first stitch over the second stitch and drop it off the needle. Carry on until all the stitches in the row have been bound off.

Shaping

I am not a fan of knitting lots of components for each toy and then having to sew them up at the end. I like to see the toy develop as it is being knitted. Therefore, my patterns have been created with shaping (increasing and decreasing stitches). This gives you a three-dimensional effect without all the sewing. I have used several shaping techniques, which are explained below.

Decreasing stitches

Decreasing stitches is where you lose a stitch. This can be achieved in several ways.

SKPO (SLIP ONE, KNIT ONE, PASS THE SLIPPED STITCH OVER)

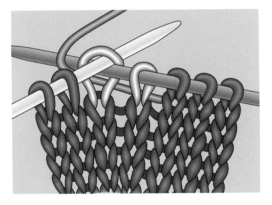

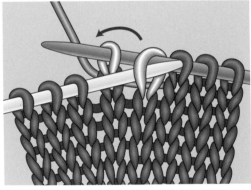

1 Knit along the row until you reach the area you want to decrease. Slip the stitch (unknitted) onto the right-hand needle. Knit the next stitch.

2 Lift the slipped stitch over the knitted stitch and off the needle. This decreases by one stitch.

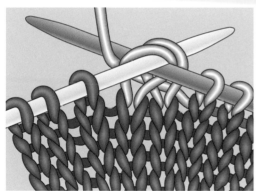

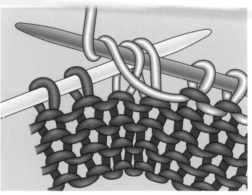

K2TOG (KNIT TWO STITCHES TOGETHER)

Knit along the row until you reach the area you want to decrease. Knit through the next two stitches as though they were one stitch. This decreases by one stitch.

P2TOG (PURL TWO STITCHES TOGETHER)

Purl along the row until you reach the area you want to decrease. Purl through the next two stitches as though they were one stitch. This decreases by one stitch.

MULTIPLE DECREASES

You can decrease by more than one stitch at a time. Some of the pattern instructions ask you to k3tog, p3tog and even p5tog. Work these decreases as explained above; you will just need to insert your working needle through three (or five) stitches and knit or purl them together as though they were one stitch. K3tog and p3tog decrease by two stitches; p5tog decreases by four stitches.

105

Increasing stitches

Increasing stitches is where you make a stitch.

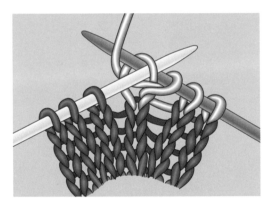

KFB (KNIT INTO THE FRONT AND BACK)
Knit along the row until you reach the area you want to increase. Knit into the front of the stitch on the left-hand needle. Instead of removing it from the needle (as with a normal knitted stitch), knit into it again through the back loop. Then slip the original stitch off the left-hand needle.

YON (YARN OVER/YARN OVER NEEDLE)
The lace panel for Polly Dolly's white dress (pp. 50–51) features another way of shaping. To make the lacy pattern you will need to pair yarnovers (a way of adding a stitch) with 'psso', or pass the slipped stitch over (a way of losing a stitch).

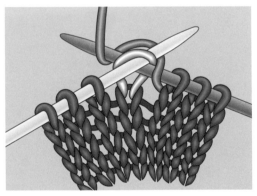

Bring the yarn over between the two needles. Knit the next stitch, taking the yarn over the right needle. This creates an extra stitch and also creates a hole in the knitted fabric.

Knitting in the round

Most of the toys in this book are knitted using two straight knitting needles, so you need to sew a seam up the back afterwards to make up the toy. However, some of the projects suggest that you knit in the round, using either a circular needle or double-pointed needles.

Knitting on a circular needle

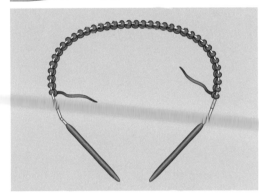

A circular needle consists of two pointed ends joined together by a flexible cord. This type of needle enables you to knit a tube of material seamlessly. Circular needles are great for knitting tubular pieces as you need to for Simon Snake (pp. 54–57). It saves you having to sew up a very long and fiddly seam afterwards. Circular needles are available in different lengths. As the snake is a narrow tube, use the shortest circular needle you can find.

Cast on as you would normally and spread the stitches along the entire length of the needle, including the flexible cord. Sometimes there are not enough stitches to reach each end, but the beauty of the flexible cord is that you can bend it through some of the stitches so that they meet. You may want to place a marker (a piece of scrap yarn will be fine) to mark the start of the round.

If you knit every round you make a tube of stockinette stitch; there's no need to turn the work or to work any purl rounds. Try to ensure that the first round is not twisted.

Knitting on double-pointed needles

I've suggested working on double-pointed needles to work the tip of Simon Snake's tail, and also to work the anchor on The Owl and the Pussycat's boat (pp. 94–95).

Double-pointed needles are shorter than standard needles and are easier to handle than a circular needle when you have only a few stitches to work on when working in the round.

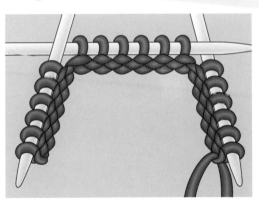

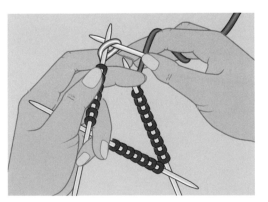

1 Cast on as you would normally and distribute the stitches equally over three double-pointed needles.

2 Continue knitting round, transferring the stitches along each needle so that you have an equal number of stitches on each needle. Again, you may want to place a marker at the beginning of the round.

Colourwork

There are two main ways to knit designs using two or more colours: Fair Isle and intarsia. Fair Isle is used to produce small-scale, intricate colour patterns, often using repeated motifs. You usually use two colours of yarn in a single row of knitting, and these yarns are stranded (carried) across the row at the back of the work. Consequently, Fair Isle fabric is double-layered. Intarsia is used to create larger chunks or blocks of colour. You will need a separate ball of yarn for each colour, and you will often have to change colours in the middle of a row. The yarns are not stranded at the back of the work, so intarsia fabric is single-layered.

Intarsia

Intarsia knitting is used for designs where there are big blocks of colour. Separate balls of wool are used for each block; unlike with Fair Isle no floats (or strands) of yarn are created at the back of the work. Intarsia colourwork is used in quite a few of the designs: Bertie and Beatrice the Birds (pp. 14–19), Frederick the Frog Prince (pp. 22–27), the Babushkas (pp. 28–33), the tails of the Three Little Fish (pp. 74–77), Peter Penguin (pp. 78–83) and the Owl (pp. 88–91).

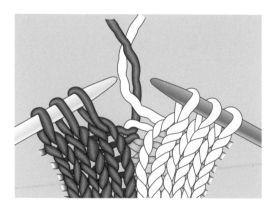

Knit along the row until the new colour is needed. Drop the first colour and pick up the second colour underneath the first colour, crossing the two colours over before knitting the next stitch in the second colour. The crossing of the stitches ensures that no holes are created between colours.

Fair Isle

Fair Isle knitting is used on more complicated coloured patterns with small, repeated motifs. I have used a Fair Isle pattern on Simon Snake's body (pp. 54–57). There is also Fair Isle patterning around the middle of the Three Little Fish body (pp. 74–77).

In Fair Isle knitting, each ball of wool is kept in action; you never cut the wool between stitches. I look in strands are created as you work; these are horizontal strands of yarn that lie on the reverse side of the knitted fabric.

Knit along the row in your first colour until you come to the stitch where you need to change colour. To knit a stitch in your second colour, put the right-hand needle through the next stitch, pulling the new coloured yarn through as the stitch. This will create a float. It is important not to pull the stitches too tightly when working on the next stitch or the knitted fabric will be distorted.

The best way to work Fair Isle is to hold one colour yarn in your right hand (usually the background colour) and the other colour yarn in your left hand.

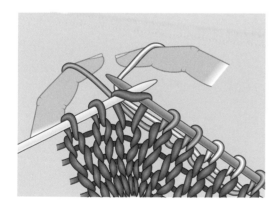

1 When knitting with the right-hand colour, keep the left-hand colour below the needle and out of the way of the working yarn.

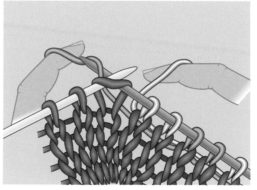

2 When knitting with the left-hand colour, keep the right-hand colour above the needle.

FAIR ISLE CHARTS
Fair Isle patterns are usually shown on a chart because it makes it easier to see how the pattern should look. You start at the bottom of the chart and work up. Each line represents a new row of knitting. Every time a coloured-in square is shown, you change colour.

The chart for Simon Snake is on p. 117, the chart for the pattern on the Three Little Fish is on p. 118.

Making up

All the patterns have been designed with the minimum amount of sewing, but there is always some sewing to be done! There are several ways to sew up knitting, so use whichever method you find easiest. Always use the same yarn you knitted with so the stitches are less visible. Darning or tapestry needles with a large eye and blunt end are best so that you don't split the yarn.

Weaving in ends

You will have some loose yarn ends from casting on and binding off, so weave these in first. One of the best ways to weave in the loose ends so they will be invisible is to thread the yarn end through a darning needle and sew it into the seam by passing the needle through the 'bumps' of the stitches on the wrong side of the work. Sew them in for about 1–2in (2.5–5cm) and then snip off any excess yarn.

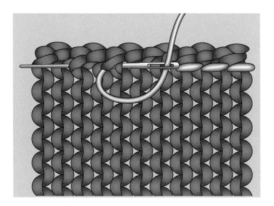

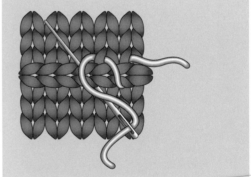

Backstitch (reverse sides out)

Put both knit sides (right sides) together so the wrong sides are facing you. Carefully make small running stitches along the edge, one stitch at a time. Make sure you are sewing in a straight line as close to the edge as possible. It might sound obvious, but it is very easy to pick up stitches that are further away from the edge than you thought. You want the sewing to be as invisible as possible.

Slip stitch (knit sides out)

Put the two pieces of knitting one above the other, knit sides out. Run the thread through the centre of the first stitch on the top piece of knitting then down through the centre of the first stitch on the bottom piece of knitting. Next go through the second stitch on the top piece of knitting and down through the centre of the bottom second stitch. Continue in this way along the row.

Stuffing the toys

Toy stuffing is an essential component for toys. Don't stuff the toys too fully or they will become solid and have no movement. You want the toys to be cuddly. Some of the projects require you to stuff the toys as you go along. This is generally when the toy is long and narrow, such as Simon Snake (pp. 54–57). This ensures you distribute an even amount of stuffing throughout the toy.

The stuffing I use is Minicraft Supersoft Toy Stuffing. It comes in bags of 250g (about 9oz) and is made of 100% polyester. If you can't find this particular brand, other suitable brands should be available at haberdashery and craft stores. It is best to use stuffing designed especially for toys so that you can be sure that it is safe for children. Check for the safety logo before you buy it.

I always use my hands to put the stuffing in the toys. You can use your fingers to push the stuffing into small or fiddly pieces.

Sewing in final ends

Once you have stuffed the toy, you will need to close the small gap in the middle of the seam. I knot together the two ends of the yarn used for sewing the seams, then thread the ends through the toy so that the knot is hidden and the ends are kept long. You don't want to cut the ends too short because it makes the knot more likely to come undone.

Finishing touches

One of the best parts about making toys is adding the finishing touches and really bringing the toys to life. It is amazing what adding a pair of beady eyes or a little pink nose can do. Here I've outlined a few techniques for sewing facial features. I also look at adding the little fabric appliqués that some of the toys have, and other little details like crocheted tails and pompoms.

Embroidering details

Spend time making the facial features perfect. It is really effective at making the toys characterful. You can use leftover bits of yarn from previous projects. You can use any sewing stitches to create these features; there really is no rule. You need the stitches to be as firm as possible so that they don't undo and look neat as well. You could use backstitch for the mouth of the pussycat (pp. 92-93) or Frederick the Frog Prince (pp. 22-27), or a single running stitch sewn over and over itself to create the shape of a large eye. You could use a French knot to make the eyes on the smaller toys if you find this easier. Choose what works best for you.

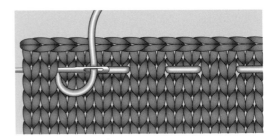

RUNNING STITCH
This is a very simple stitch. Thread a darning or tapestry needle with the yarn you want to use and insert it from the back of the work through to the front where you want the stitch to start. Insert it back through your knitting where you want your stitch to end. This creates an effect like a line of dashes.

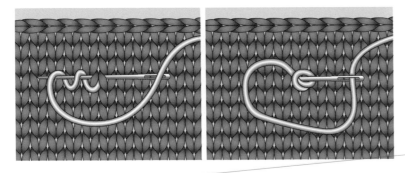

FRENCH KNOT
Bring the needle from the back to the front of the work and wind the yarn twice round the needle. Pull the needle through the twists bringing the yarn through too. This creates the knot. You can twist the yarn round the needle more times if you want a bigger knot and once only for a smaller knot.

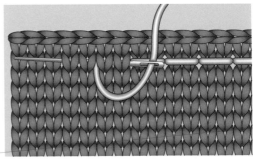

BACKSTITCH
Sew a running stitch to create the pattern you want. Once you have reached the end of your pattern go back on yourself, filling in the gaps between the stitches. This should create one single line.

Appliqués

A large number of the projects combine knitting with fabric appliqués; for example, the fabric patches sewn under the birds' wings or in the teddies' ears. I think this adds a special character to the toys and brings out the nostalgic, personalized nature of the work. You can use cherished pieces of fabric set aside for a special project. Toys provide you with the perfect reason to use such fabrics.

IRON-ON INTERFACING
Iron-on interfacing is perfect for lining your fabric. It stops the edges from fraying and makes the fabric more solid, thereby enabling you to cut out small shapes like the foot pads, ear pads or flower shapes. You can buy iron-on interfacing from most haberdashery stores; Vilene is a popular brand.

When using the iron-on interfacing, I cut out a piece that is bigger than the template. I then iron this piece onto the fabric and peel off the paper. The interfacing makes the fabric stiffer so it is easier to cut out the shape.

Hold the cut-out piece onto the toy and sew round the edges. If you find it easier, you could pin the cut-out piece to the toy before sewing it on.

SEWING THE FABRIC ON
There are several ways you can sew the fabric details onto the knitting. Try to get your stitching as neat as possible and be creative with the colour of thread you use. The most important thing to ensure is that the fabric is sewn securely to the knitting. Use normal sewing thread rather than yarn.

Crochet chains

Some of the toys feature crocheted chains; Eddie Elephant, the piggies and the mice have crochet-chain tails, while the birds have crochet-chain legs. Crocheting a chain is quite simple.

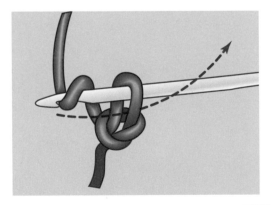

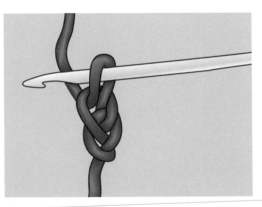

1 Tie a slipknot in the working end of the yarn and place the loop on your crochet hook. Wrap the yarn clockwise over the hook.

2 Pull the yarn through the loop on the hook to form a fresh loop. This is the first chain. Repeat the process until the chain is as long as you want it.

114

Pompoms

Pompoms are used for the tails of the bunnies. They are very simple to make. You can buy pompom kits that make the process quicker, but here are instructions for the old-fashioned way.

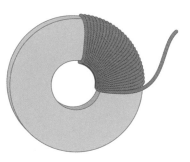

1 Using the template on p. 116, cut out two pieces of card. Remember to cut out the centre hole too. Wrap the wool in and out of the centre hole, working your way around the pompom ring.

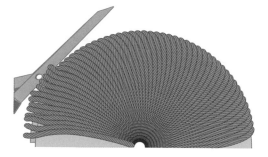

2 Continue wrapping the wool around the ring until it completely covers all the card. Carefully cut round the edge of the pompom. The two rings of card mean you can slip your scissors between the rings to make cutting easier.

3 Pull the two pieces of card slightly apart and slip a piece of string around the pompom centre. Wrap the string round a few times and knot tightly. It is important to wrap tightly to ensure that the pompom doesn't fall apart. Slip out the pieces of card (cut them if you need to).

Your pompom is complete. Trim round the edge to create a perfectly round ball with no longer tufty bits of yarn.

Templates

THE BUNNY BUNCH
(PP. 10–13)

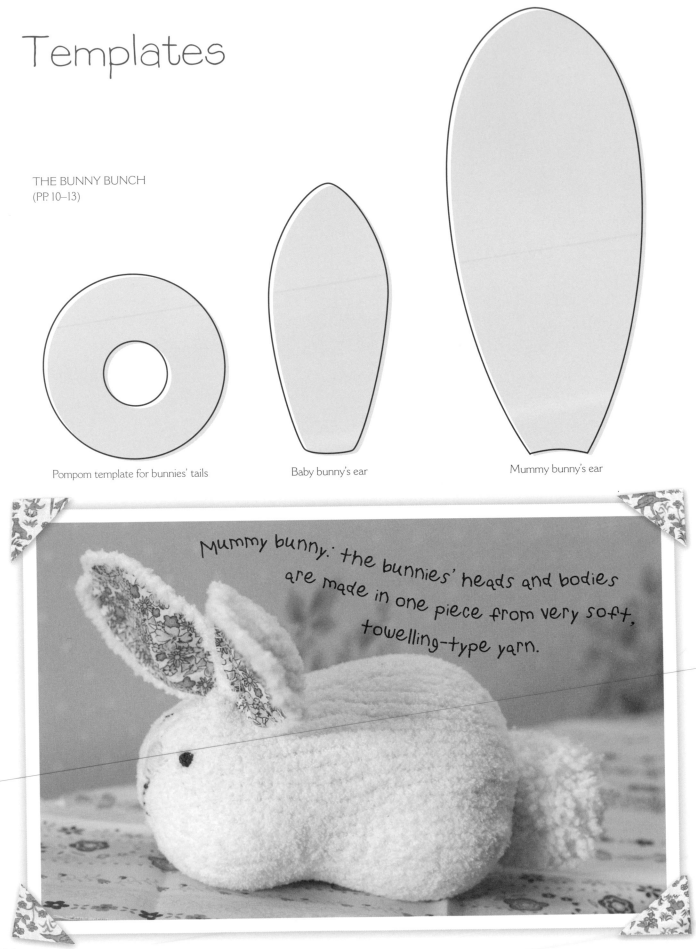

Pompom template for bunnies' tails

Baby bunny's ear

Mummy bunny's ear

Mummy bunny: the bunnies' heads and bodies are made in one piece from very soft, towelling-type yarn.

SIMON SNAKE (PP. 54–57)

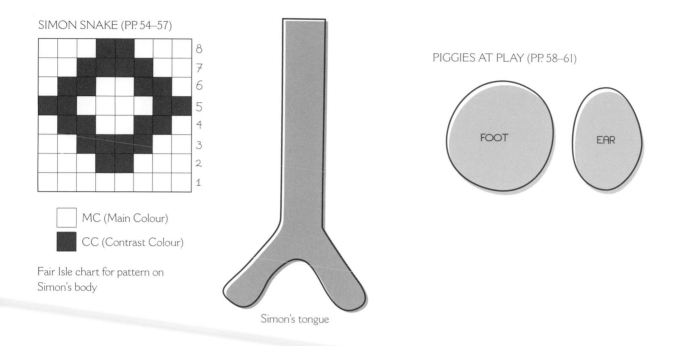

8
7
6
5
4
3
2
1

☐ MC (Main Colour)

■ CC (Contrast Colour)

Fair Isle chart for pattern on Simon's body

Simon's tongue

PIGGIES AT PLAY (PP. 58–61)

FOOT

EAR

THE OWL AND THE PUSSYCAT (PP. 86–95)

Owl's eye

Pussycat's ear

THREE LITTLE FISH (P.P. 74–77)

Three colourways for the fish

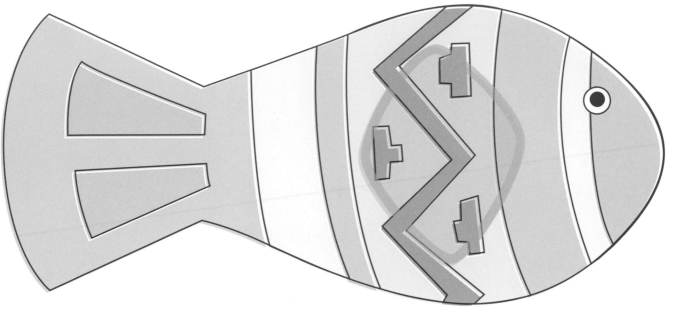

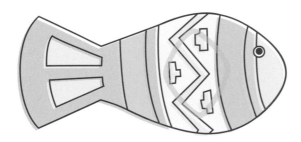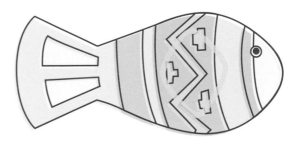

Fair Isle chart for pattern on the pink
finned fish's body

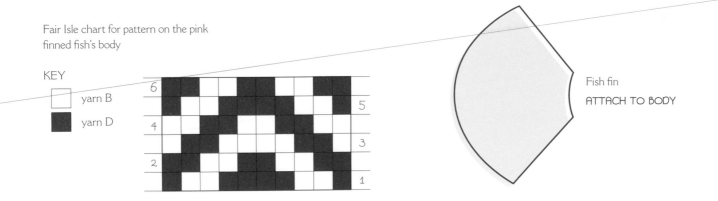

KEY

☐	yarn B
■	yarn D

Fish fin
ATTACH TO BODY

BERTIE AND BEATRICE THE BIRDS
(PP. 14–19)

Bird's wing

EDDIE THE FRIENDLY ELEPHANT (PP. 68–73)

Elephant's ear

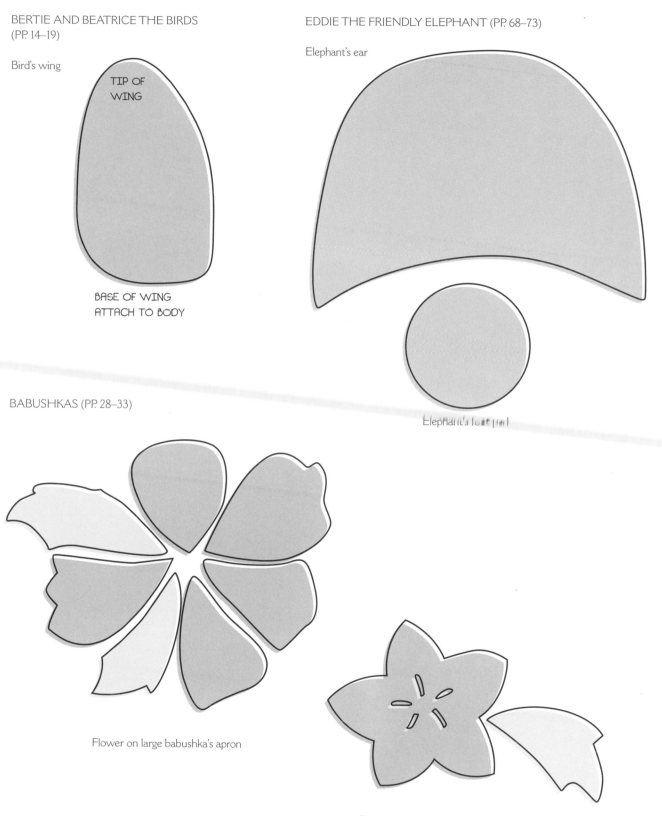

TIP OF
WING

BASE OF WING
ATTACH TO BODY

Elephant's foot [pad]

BABUSHKAS (PP. 28–33)

Flower on large babushka's apron

Flower on medium babushka's apron

POLLY DOLLY'S DRESS-UP DAY (P.P. 42–51)

Flower on Polly's white dress

Polly's knickers

TOP

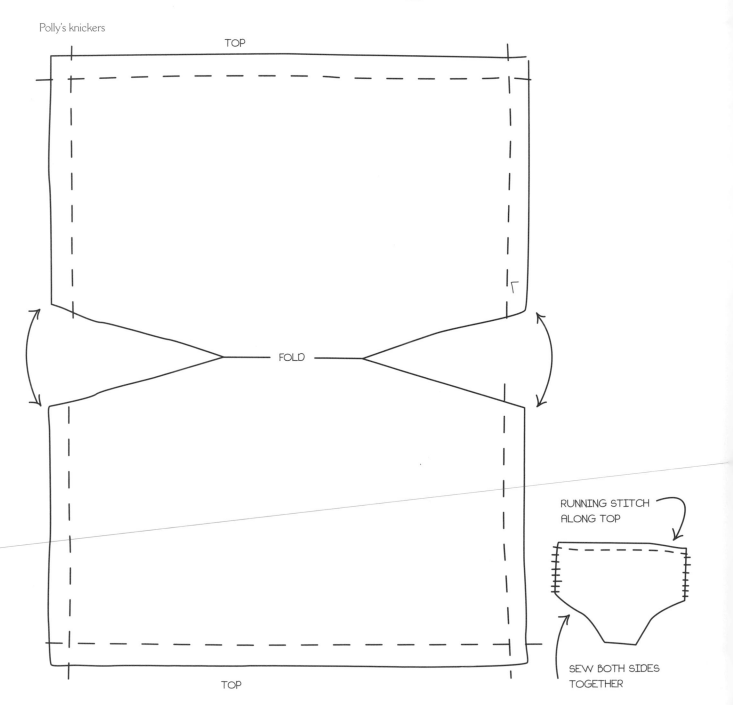

FOLD

TOP

RUNNING STITCH
ALONG TOP

SEW BOTH SIDES
TOGETHER

Polly's vest

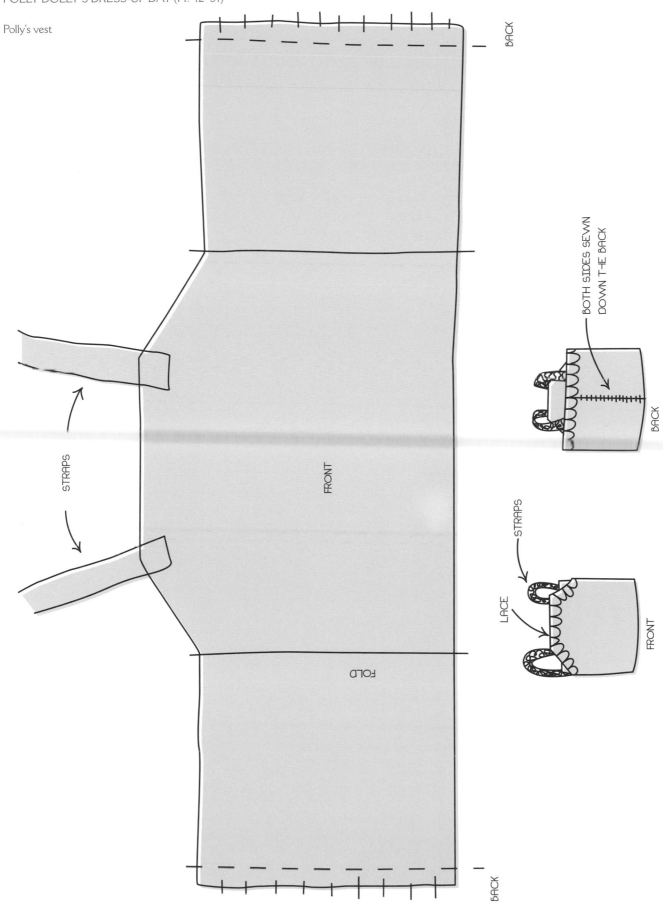

THREE HUNGRY BEARS (P.P. 36–41)

Mummy teddy

Daddy teddy

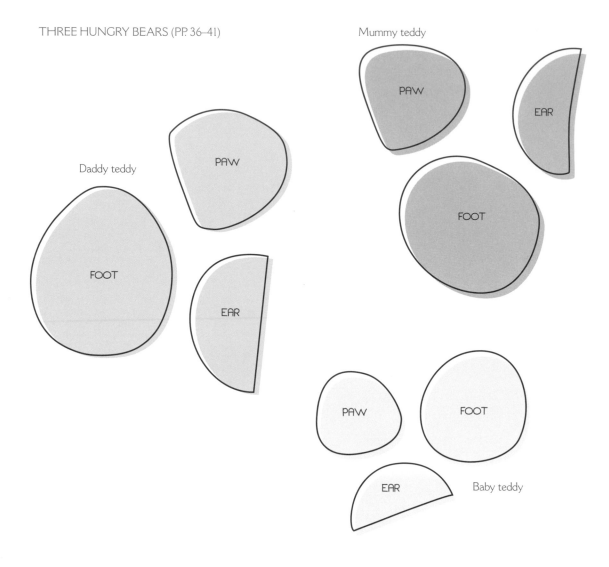

PAW

EAR

FOOT

PAW

FOOT

EAR

PAW

FOOT

EAR

Baby teddy

FREDERICK THE FROG PRINCE (P.P. 22–27)

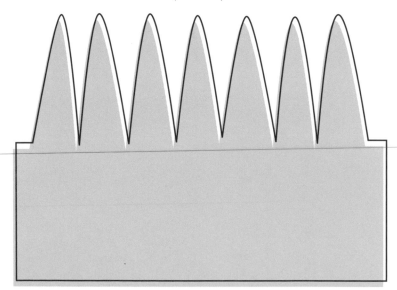

Frederick's crown

Yarns used

In the project instructions I have given a generic description of the yarn used for the project so you can easily source a yarn to use or pick something suitable out of your stash. However, if you want to recreate the project exactly, I have specified the yarns used below.

Be warned that yarn companies frequently update their lines, so they may discontinue a certain type of yarn or a certain colour. If the yarns specified below become unavailable, or if you want to use a substitute yarn, you will need to work out how much replacement yarn you need – the meterage or yardage of a ball of yarn can vary considerably between lines and between brands. Make this calculation:
- **The number of balls of the recommended yarn x the number of yards/metres per ball = A.**
- **The number of yards/metres per ball of the substitute yarn = B.**
- **Divide A by B to calculate the number of balls of substitute yarn required.**

Many of the projects use only small amounts of yarn, so you may only need one or two balls of yarn anyway.

PAGE 10 THE BUNNY BUNCH

Peter Pan Darling DK (100% polyester; 122yd/112m per 1¾oz/50g ball)

MUMMY BUNNY
1 ball in colour 360 (**A**)

BABY BOY BUNNY
1 ball in each of colours 360 (**A**) and 365 (**B**)

BABY GIRL BUNNY
1 ball in colour 363 (**C**)

(NB: 1 ball of **A** is enough to make both the mummy bunny and the face of the baby boy bunny)

PAGE 14 BERTIE AND BEATRICE THE BIRDS

Patons Fairytale Colour 4 Me DK (100% wool; 95yd/90m per 1¾oz/50g ball)

BERTIE BIRD
1 ball in each of colours 4955 (**A**), 4960 (**B**) and 4952 (**C**)

BEATRICE BIRD
1 ball in each of colours 4958 (**A**), 4960 (**B**) and 4955 (**C**)

PAGE 22 FREDERICK THE FROG PRINCE

(**A**) Twilleys of Stamford Freedom Spirit (100% wool; 131yd/120m per 1¾oz/50g ball)
1 ball in colour 514
(**B**) Patons Fairytale Colour 4 Me DK (100% wool; 95yd/90m per 1¾oz/50g ball)
1 ball in colour 4952
(**C**) Oddment of yarn in white
(**D**) Oddment of yarn in black

PAGE 28 BABUSHKAS

Sirdar Country Style DK (45% acrylic, 40% nylon, 15% wool; 348yd/318m per 3½oz/100g ball)
1 ball in each of colours 593 (**A**), 584 (**B**), 412 (**C**) and 402 (**D**)

PAGE 36 THREE HUNGRY BEARS

Rowan RYC Baby Alpaca DK (100% baby alpaca; 109yd/100m per 1¾oz/50g ball)

MUMMY BEAR
1 ball in colour 206

DADDY BEAR
2 balls in colour 205

BABY BEAR
1 ball in colour 202

Suppliers

Below are some contact details for the suppliers of yarns that I used for making the toys.

SIRDAR

www.sirdar.co.uk

(USA) Knitting Fever Inc.
315 Bayview Avenue
Amityville, NY 11701
Tel: +1 516 546 3600
www.knittingfever.com

(UK) Sirdar Spinning Ltd
Flanshaw Lane, Alvethorpe
Wakefield WF2 9ND
Tel: +44 (0)1924 371501
email: enquiries@sirdar.co.uk

(AUS) Creative Images
PO Box 106
Hastings, Victoria 3915
Tel: +61 (0)3 5979 1555
email: creative@peninsula.starway.net.au

CYGNET

www.cygnetyarns.com
Cygnet Yarns Ltd
12-14 Adelaide Street
Bradford
West Yorkshire
BD5 0EF
Tel: +44 (0)1274 743374
www.cygnetyarns·co·uk

TWILLEYS

www.twilleys.co.uk

(UK) Twilleys of Stamford
For craft/haberdashery:
Roman Mill, Stamford PE9 1BG
Tel: +44 (0)1780 752661
email: twilleys@tbramsden.co.uk

For head office, administration, handknitting,
industrial yarns and shade fringes:
Thomas B· Ramsden (Bradford) Ltd,
Netherfiield Road, Guiseley, Leeds LS20 9PD
Tel: +44 (0)1943 872264
email: sales@tbramsden.co.uk

(note: **also suppliers of Peter Pan Darling DK**)

ROWAN

www.knitrowan.com

(USA) Westminster Fibers Inc
165 Ledge Street, Nashua
New Hampshire 03060
Tel: +1 603 886 5041/5043
www.westminsterfibers.com
email: info@westminsterfibers.com

(UK) Rowan
Green Lane Mill, Holmfirth HD9 2DX
Tel: +44 (0)1484 681881
email: info@knitrowan.com

(AUS) Australian Country Spinners Pty Ltd
Level 7, 409 St Kilda Road
Melbourne, Victoria 3004
Tel: +61 (0)3 9380 3888
email: tkohut@auspinners.com.au

PATONS

www.coatscrafts.co.uk

(USA/CAN) 320 Livingstone Avenue South
Listowel, ON, N4W 3H3
Canada
Tel: +1 888 368 8401
www.patonsyarns.com
email: inquire@patonsyarns.com

(UK) Coats Crafts UK
PO Box 22, Lingfield House
Lingfield Point, McMullen Road
Darlington DL1 1YJ
Tel: +44 (0)1325 394237
www.coatscrafts.co.uk
email: consumer.ccuk@coats.com

(AUS) Patons
PO Box 7276, Melbourne Victoria 3004
Tel: +61 (0)3 9380 3888
www.patons.bi3
email: enquiries@auspinners.com.au

About the author

Laura Long graduated in 2003 with a First Class knitted textiles degree from Central St. Martins College of Art and Design. Since then she has been working out of her central London studio designing, making and selling her knitted creations to boutiques and galleries all over the world. Teaching and freelance work has played an important part in her business. She designs, makes and creates patterns and pieces for designers, knitting magazines and pattern books, and her clients have included John Rocha, Rowan yarns, *Simply Knitting* and *Knit Today* magazines, and publications such as *Collective Knitting* and *Holiday Knits*.
She has taught both machine and hand knitting to people of all ages at Greenwich Community College, Loop, and the Cockpit Arts.

Dolls, fairytales and fantasy played an important part in Laura's childhood, a childhood full of happy, everlasting memories.
It is for this reason that she has developed a collection of childhood characters, knitted creatures and dolls with a personality all of their own.

Acknowledgments

Thank you to everyone at David and Charles, particularly Jennifer Fox-Proverbs, Prudence Rogers, Sabine Eulau, Sarah Underhill, Bethany Dymond and Kate Nicholson for all their amazing work and support. Thank you Sian Irvine for bringing my characters to life - your photography is fantastic! I would also like to thank all the yarn companies for the fantastic yarns they have supplied.

Index